The Illustrated History of the

Naval Stores (Turpentine) Industry

With Artifact Value Guide, Home Remedies, Recipes and Jokes

By Pete Gerrell

SYP (Southern Yellow Pine) Publishing
P.O. Box 627
Crawfordville, Fl 32326

The Illustrated History
of the
NAVAL STORES (TURPENTINE)
INDUSTRY

The Illustrated History of the Naval Stores Industry is a culmination of many years of enjoyable research by the author. Tracing the history of the industry from Biblical times through the years until its end in the 1970's the author has, for the first time, portrayed the story behind the industry from beginning to end.

Copyright TXU 814-159 1997 by Pete Gerrell

First Edition, Aug. 1998
Second Printing, 1999

ISBN
Library of Congress Catalog Card No. 98-90418

SYP (Southern Yellow Pine) Publishing
P.O. Box 627
Crawfordville, FL 32326
TGANTIQUE2@prodigy.net

Printed in the USA by

MORRIS PUBLISHING
3212 East Highway 30 • Kearney, NE 68847 • 1-800-650-7888

Acknowledgments

It is not possible to thank all of the people in writing that have inspired me in this work through the years. There are four people that I feel deserve a very special thanks for their help and patience.

My wife, Terri, who has been my co-pilot, or should I say, co-digger, in the excavating and restoration of many of the articles pictured in this book.

My mother, who has traveled with me through the woods and pointed out the location of many old camp, still, home and school sites that she remembers from her childhood some 70 plus years ago.

Robin Breg, who has, to my good fortune, taken a very personal interest in making sure that this work got completed. Robin had the largest job of all, listening to my southern country voice on tape and translating it to computer.

My son, Allen, who reproduced from old pictures or my memory any old tool or implement that I couldn't otherwise find.

Thank you so very much, all!

INTRODUCTION

I've put off the writing of this book for several years because I've enjoyed doing the research so much. I keep wanting to go back and do more research, but sooner or later I'm going to have to get down to putting it on paper so I can see what I've got and get it organized. I'll be rambling through, doing this as a history and, as an amateur historian, I tend to do my history in the "three R's method - rambling, reminiscing and repeating" - so a lot of this will be done that way. Maybe in the last writing of it after the drafts, I'll be able to come through and cut out some of the repeating, but probably not all of the rambling and definitely not the reminiscing.

The first thing I need to put in, and probably the most important thing, is the disclaimer - the home remedies, recipes, corny jokes, and any other writings contained in this book are provided for historical purposes only. No express or implied warranties with regards to their efficacy, safety, edibility or humor are made by the author or the publisher.

Bibliography of Sources

NSR Naval Stores Review. April 26, 1947. Weekly publication by H.L. Peace Publications, 433 W. Church St., Jacksonville, FL.

USDA Turpentine Still, Still Buildings and Equipment. Naval Stores Research Division United States Department of Agriculture. Miscellaneous Publication No. 387. 1940. U.S Government Printing Office, Washington, D.C..

FFS Florida Forest Service, Tallahassee, FL.

USDA U.S. Department of Agriculture, Forest Service, Southeastern Forest Experiment Station, Asheville, NC. April 1960 Manual Modern Gum and Naval Stores Methods.

Mc McCranie's Turpentine Still, Atkinson County, Georgia. A Historical Analysis of the Site by Kenneth Thomas, Jr. Report submitted April 30, 1975. State of Georgia, Department of Natural Resources.

SJPC St. Joseph Land and Development Co., 7945 Coastal Highway, Crawfordville, FL.

G Gamble's - International Naval Stores Year Book. Thomas Gamble, Savannah, GA.

Bonnie J. Allen - Information on CC Land and High Bluff Turpentine Co.

WT Wakulla Turpentine Company. Manufacturers of Pure Gum Turpentine and Rosin, Wakulla, FL. Miscellaneous files from trash container on St. Mark's Trail, Tallahassee, FL, 1996.

GA Georgia Agrirama, Tifton, GA. Miscellaneous Photographs.

FDS Florida Department of State, Bureau of Archives and Record Management, Tallahassee, FL. Miscellaneous Photographs.

FTIS Florida for Tourists, Invalids, and Settlers. By George M. Barbour. D. Appleton and Company, 1,3 and 5 Bond Street, New York, NY. 1882 Description of the Camp.

A Pictures taken by the author and many articles about the industry that I have stored in my memory and recalled during writing.

Cookery Recipes of Molly Hall French. Unpublished. Undated. C-1890

Farmers and Planters Almanac. 1931-1933. Published by Blum's Almanac Syndicate, Jennings, NC. Miscellaneous jokes and home remedies (with revisions by the author.)

ATFA Calendar. Catherine King, Vienna Antiques, 101 7th St. North, Vienna, GA.

James C. Morris, Chief Deputy, Decatur Co, GA Sheriff's Dept. for his contribution to the value of industry artifacts

TABLE OF CONTENTS

Industry Artifacts Value Guide

THROUGH TIME

The production of Naval Stores was always a picturesque industry with a language all its own. It is older than the lumber industry and its history reaches back to days many centuries before Christ, when the natives of Asia manufactured pitches and oils from gum or resin of the trees which grew on the shores of the Mediterranean Sea. In the early days, the gum was gathered, put into pots and cooked down to a thick mass. Over the pots while it was cooking, fleecy sheep skins were stretched, which condensed and held the rising vapors or oil distilled out of the resin. This oil was recovered by the crude method of wringing out the fleeces. Oil recovered in this way was used in some of the arts and industries. One of its interesting uses was in the manufacture of the age-enduring mummy varnish. The thick mass left in the pot was pitch. It is recorded that in building the Ark, Noah was commanded to pitch it within and without with pitch.

In this country, the collection of gum from pines and the making of pitch and tar date back to the early part of the 17th Century. However, the first records of importance are of a century later. At that time the gum was gathered from the pines of Virginia and North Carolina. It was placed in kettles and heated until most of the volatile part had been steamed off and only a pitchy mass remained. This pitch was strained and used in caulking the seams of wooden ships. With the growth of the colonies, a small Naval Stores industry grew up along the middle Atlantic coast and slowly extended south. The method and equipment were still very primitive and there was little thought of improvement or expansion of the business. Later, however, the resin obtained from the trees was shipped to distilleries located at the leading markets, such as Philadelphia, New York and London, where it was cooked in closed iron retorts. Here a portion of the volatile oil, hitherto wasted, was condensed and saved. This product was called spirits of turpentine, or oil of turpentine, and was used extensively for lighting and as a solvent for other materials. By 1850 the world was finding new uses for both turpentine and rosin, which constantly increased the demand and caused a steady growth in the industry. Rosin and spirits of turpentine, as well as the manufactured products they were used in, were being shipped into almost every country in the world. Almost two-thirds of the world's Naval Stores were produced in the southern United States. In the South, the annual value of Naval Stores was $40 million. The industry employed almost 400,000 people and paid them more than $15 million a year in wages. Four-fifths of the Naval Stores were harvested from live trees and were known as Gum Naval Stores. Turpentine and rosin were essential ingredients in many commodities. They were used in printing ink and for color printing processes and lithographs, as a preventive for bleeding, in the manufacture of cotton and wool print goods and the manufacture of patent leather, as a thinner for waxes, and leather, floor and furniture polishes, as an ingredient in belting greases, laundry glosses, washing preparations, stove polishes and sealing wax. It was a raw material for producing synthetic camphor and, indirectly, celluloid, explosives, fireworks and medicine. It was also used in making disinfectants, liniments, poultices, medicated soap, ointments and internal remedies. A large percent of the turpentine produced was used in the manufacture of paints and varnishes. Rosin was used in the manufacture of soap and for the surfacing of paper suitable for writing and printing. It was also used in the manufacture of rosin oils, varnishes, ink dryers, waterproofing compounds, roofing materials, leather dressings, shoe polishes, sealing waxes, linoleum, oil cloths, floor waxes and printing ink.

The natural range of the longleaf pine extended from Southeastern Virginia, southward over the Atlantic and Gulf coastal plains to Florida and westward to eastern Texas. The range for the slash pine extended from about Charleston, South Carolina, westward to Southern Georgia, Alabama, Mississippi and Southeastern Louisiana to the Mississippi River and southward in Florida almost to the southern extremity. Both kinds of trees came from seeds borne in cones. The young trees never sprang from the roots as do many hardwood trees. When the cones matured and opened, the seeds winged their way to the ground and, if given a chance, germinated. Before the days of planting, it was important when the trees were cut for lumber to leave a few good seed trees per acre. If the seed trees were left and the land protected from fire and piney woods rooter hogs, nature would do its part to bring back the trees. It was increasingly apparent to leaders in the industry that the permanent welfare of the Naval Stores industry demanded more careful conservation of the trees.

Parliament passed the Naval Stores Bounty Act in 1705, which created the payment of a substantial subsidy for Naval Stores production per barrel to try to encourage the industry. When the Act was renewed in 1729, the bounty was reduced to a much lower incentive because of oversupply in the Colonies.

The labor force that was needed to work the forest to gather the resin was usually employed elsewhere for most of this time, mainly on the farms and plantations which used the lumber industry during the winter to keep the workers busy, make extra money and clear the land. Since turpentine farming was year round work, it did not lend itself to being a winter or part-time occupation for the idle farm workers. Tar and pitch, on the other hand, could be curtailed in winter time and also could be used for the westward expansion needs of land clearance since these products could be obtained from tree stumps as well as trees that were not used for lumber. In 1766 the Georgia Assembly passed an Act concerning Naval Stores in an effort to bring Georgia into compliance with the Parliamentary Act of 1729. Georgia's Act specified the standards and volumes for shipping Naval Stores as well as the inspection required prior to shipment. In the twenty years prior to the Revolutionary War, Georgia exported only 877 barrels of turpentine, 2,988 barrels of pitch and 4,404 barrels of tar, placing the colony fourth behind North Carolina, which produced 60% of the colonial Naval Stores exports. Between the Revolution and the 1830s there was little change in the turpentine or Naval Stores industry. North Carolina continued to be the leading state in production, although statistics for this period are scarce. It was not until the advent of new uses and new equipment that the industry began to boom and eventually wear out and waste the pine resources of North Carolina and necessitate the move southward. Several things brought the change to the Naval Stores industry. New uses were found for turpentine and rosin. Spirits of turpentine had a greater number of uses after 1830. One major new use was as a fuel for lamps to replace whale oil. There were improvements in distillation, particularly in the innovation of the copper still in 1834. A third reason for the upswing in the industry was improved transportation capabilities in North Carolina, where most of the Industry was centered.

In 1931 a Naval Stores experiment station under the direction of the Bureau of Chemistry and Soils of the United States Department of Agriculture was established at Olustee, Florida. It was known as the Naval Stores Station. Many new findings were made that were of great value to the Naval Stores industry. In a bulletin in 1937 the important accomplishments of the Naval Stores Division of the Bureau of Chemistry and Soils were listed. A few are as follows: 1) Devised a method for making from ordinary gum a rosin product that is seven grades higher than the 13 American standard grades. 2) Was responsible for giving the industry a permanent set of standards for grading rosin, which was accepted all over the world. 3) Developed a fire still that heats easily, draws well, and saves fuel. High grades of rosin could be produced in this still. 4) Demonstrated that the use of a thermometer on a still paid the producer in better grades of rosin. 5) Proved that raw gum contaminated with iron rust from rusty cups and gutters could lower the quality of rosin as much as three or four grades. 6) Developed a new type of steam turpentine still with increased capacity and productivity. 7) Devised a method for improving pine gum. 8) Through cooperation with state organizations, made available to producers the best practices in still operation.

The amount of gum that was produced by a tree of any given size was affected by many factors. In the early 1930's, studies were conducted by the United States Forest Service to determine the effect of some of those factors on yields. The following were the most important factors that influenced the total gum yield of a tree: 1) size of the tree, 2) rate of growth of a tree, 3) crown development, 4) weather conditions, particularly air temperature, 5) method of chipping, 6) geographic location of the tree, 7) the width of the face, 8) the sharpness of the chipping tools used. Records of yields of trees of various diameters from a number of points in Georgia and Florida were combined and formed the basis of Table I. The yields were from trees that were worked one face per tree. The figures in the table represent the approximate range of yields for timber of the diameters given. Since it is a composite of a large number of yield records from many points, a crowded stand of slow growing timber on a poor site will fall in the poor class, whereas very vigorous heavy-topped trees will fall in the good class. Heavily overcupped crops would not give those averages, nor would heavy back cupping operations.

Table I

There were 13 grades of rosin that were based on color and clarity. The best grades were those that were the palest and clearest. There was considerable difference in the price paid for the poorest and the best grades, which is shown on Table II. The market quotations on Table II were those of February 1, 1938 in Savannah, Georgia. The official grades were known by the letters of the alphabet. The names in the second column of the table were trade names applied to them.

At last the happy day arrived. Just before she was dressed for the ceremony, Gracie, the hand who was to be the bride that night, came to her employer. She said, "Miss Kate, will you do me a favor?" "Of course, Gracie, what is it?" "I've got $4.50, Miss Kate, will you keep it for me until tomorrow?" "Why yes, but I thought you were going to get married tonight." "Well I am, ma'am, but you don't expect I'm going to have all that money in my room and me sleeping with a strange man?"

TABLE 1
Turpentine Yields per Crop
(Yields for 32- Streak Season)
(Crop is 10,000 Faces)

Diameter at Breast Height of Tree	SLASH			LONGLEAF		
	Poor Site	Medium Site	Good Site	Poor Site	Medium Site	Good Site
Inches	bbls	bbls	bbls	bbls	bbls	bbls
9	33	40	47	32	38	44
10	39	46	54	37	43	51
11	46	53	62	42	49	58
12	52	61	69	47	56	65

TABLE 2
Prices of Rosin by Grades
(Savannah, GA - Feb 1, 1938)

Official Grade	Names Often Used By Industry	Price*	Percent of Receipts of ** Each Grade At Savannah And Jacksonville, 1928 - 30
X	Extra	$7.80	4.3
WW	Water White	$7.80	4.3
WG	Window Glass	$7.10	4.5
N	Nancy	$6.05	7.7
M	Mary	$5.95	11.8
K	Kate	$5.80	15.6
I	Isaac	$5.80	17.8
H	Harry	$5.80	17
G	George	$5.70	9.4
F	Frank	$5.65	5.5
E	Edward	$4.65	3.4
D	Dolly	$4.60	3
B	Bob	$4.60	

*Price quotations on Rosin were always given on barrels of 280 pounds.
It was actually contained in "round" barrels of 500 pounds gross or 420
pounds net weight.
**Gamble's International Naval Stores Year Book

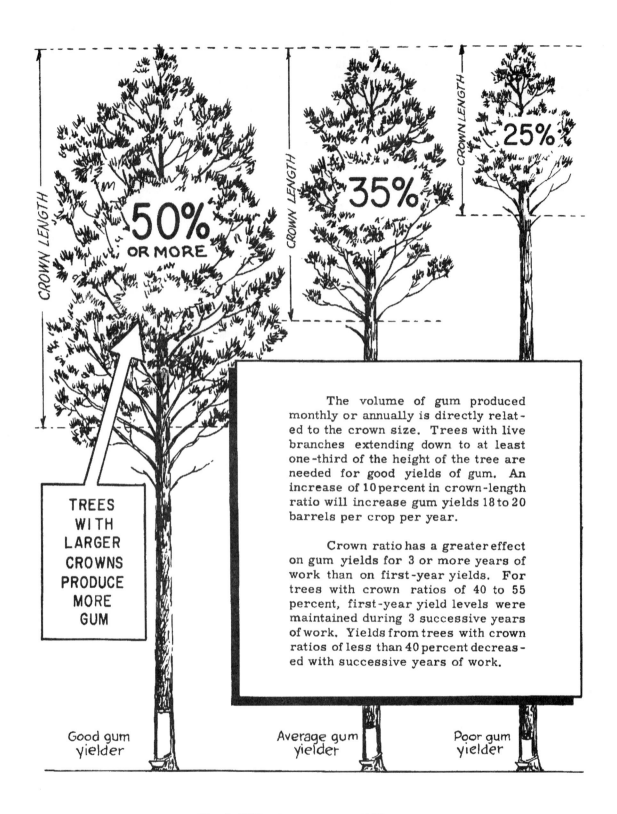

CROWN LENGTH

CROWN LENGTH

CROWN LENGTH

50% OR MORE

35%

25%

TREES WITH LARGER CROWNS PRODUCE MORE GUM

The volume of gum produced monthly or annually is directly related to the crown size. Trees with live branches extending down to at least one-third of the height of the tree are needed for good yields of gum. An increase of 10 percent in crown-length ratio will increase gum yields 18 to 20 barrels per crop per year.

Crown ratio has a greater effect on gum yields for 3 or more years of work than on first-year yields. For trees with crown ratios of 40 to 55 percent, first-year yield levels were maintained during 3 successive years of work. Yields from trees with crown ratios of less than 40 percent decreased with successive years of work.

Good gum yielder

Average gum yielder

Poor gum yielder

How to keep meat and fish from going bad after it's cooked: put a few pieces of charcoal into the saucepan wherein the fish or meat is to be boiled.

How to keep boiled fish firm Add a little saltpeter to the water in which the fish is to be boiled, 1/4 ounce to 1 gallon.

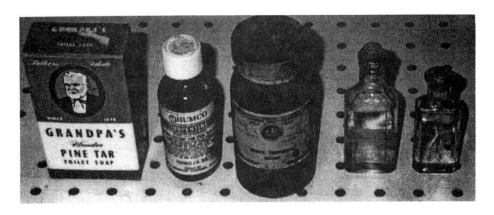

Two bottles of turpentine. The bottle on the right is pure turpentine. The bottle on the left is pure turpentine on top and water on the bottom. This indicates how the turpentine floats and separates automatically from the water. Also pictured are bottles of turpentine gum spirits used for medical purposes and a cake of "Grandpa's pine tar soap." (A)

Looking down into the rosin barrel at a piece of rosin. Notice the dark color of the piece, which indicates that it was not a good grade. The lighter color of the rosin in the barrel below the piece indicates that it is a good grade. The quality of rosin depended on the care and skill which marked every step, from the tree to the shipping container. To make high grade rosin the gum had to be free from pine needles, chips, trash and dirt. The still's heat had to be regulated with great accuracy to produce the best results. If the gum got too hot it would discolor through the scorching of the chips that were in the charge. Rusty cups discolored the raw gum and caused the rosin produced from it to be a darker color, thus lowering the grade. Rosin varied in color from black to pale lemon yellow. The grades were based not only on color, but on clarity, the palest, clearest grades being the highest priced. (GA)

American Turpentine Farmer's Association
AT-FA

Research indicates that the AT-FA was originally formed in the late 1920's, however it must not have been active during the Depression years. It appears to have been reorganized in 1936 with the first annual meeting being held in Valdosta, Georgia that year.

The green AT-FA advertising label was first used in an ad campaign in 1939. The advertising was "aimed directly at the housewives, home builders and the little man who needs a can of paint thinner."

The ad campaign must not have produced the needed results. "Competition was too keen from the lower-priced mineral spirits which flooded the post-war market."

There were approximately 500 producers, processors, factors and distributors at the 11th annual meeting in Valdosta, GA on April 16, 1947. They met at the Ritz Theater to hear Judge Harley Langdale, Association President, present the annual report.

The following excerpts from the 11th Annual Convention of the American Turpentine Farmers Association, meeting in Valdosta, GA, April 26, 1947 will tend to show you the feared downfall of the industry at that time.

"During the meeting at the Ritz Theater, the ballot of the election of the Board of Directors of the Association were counted and it was announced that all had been reelected. They are Judge Langdale; R.M. Newton, Wiggins, MS; W. L. Rose, Esdell SC; A.V. Kennedy, Waycross, GA; J. L. Giles, Jr., Soperton, GA; C.V. Mise,

Gainesville, FL; V.G. Phillips, Tallahassee, FL; R.M. Reynolds, Bainbridge, GA and M.C. Stallworth, Jr., Vinegar Bend, AL.

The following day the Board of Directors of the Association reelected the same officers, who are Judge Langdale, President, R.M. Newton, Vice President, J. Lundie Smith, Secretary and General Counsel, Ora B. Hemmingway, Treasurer and Assistant Secretary.

The increase in assessments agreed upon at the meeting require that every processor pay $1.00 instead of $.50 for each unit of Gum Naval Stores that he produces and that every producer pay $.20 instead of $.10 for each barrel of crude gum that he produces. Judge Langdale, in his report, pointed out that even with the limited budget available the national advertising campaign promoting turpentine in small containers brought results that were immediate and phenomenal. He said that from a price of 17.5 cents a gallon in 1939, when the advertising campaign was begun turpentine advanced in a steady march. "The gum industry faces able, aggressive and intelligent competition from many new spirits companies," stated the Association President. " This competition must be met by the gum industry," he added, "or the industry will be swallowed up by it. These and other types of competitive products can be produced more cheaply than gum turpentine," said the Judge. "Since the bulk of gum turpentine cost lies in labor," he pointed out, " it is obvious that gum turpentine cannot compete on a price basis. If it competes at all," he emphasized," it is going to have to do so on a basis of superiority and merit. While everyone in the industry knows of the superiority of gum turpentine," continued the Judge, "the vital fact before the Association is that all outsiders, everybody, must be told this story.

And I know but one way to do that," he said, "advertise, advertise, advertise, and then advertise some more."

Judge Langdale, speaking briefly at a luncheon the next day, welcomed the visitors and said that the members of the Association were glad to have the opportunity to take them on a field trip to show them that Gum Naval Stores is not a doomed industry. He pointed out that the first cargo ship ever to leave this country, on its return to England, bore Naval Stores. He also said that today there are counties in the belt where the bread and butter of entire families comes entirely from their earnings in working with Gum Naval Stores.

Judge Harley W. Langdale, President of the American Turpentine Farmer's Association, in his annual report last week asked for additional revenues to advertise the product throughout the nation. Members of the Association, answering that call to arms, voted unanimously to increase dues to $.20 per barrel of gum. "To meet the onslaught of aggressive and intelligent low priced competition, the industry must double and redouble its advertising campaign," Langdale told the members at its annual meeting in Valdosta. "Otherwise, the gum turpentine industry is doomed," said the prominent producer. "We have come to the crossroads," he declared, "with the world again becoming a buyer's market. There is going to be a great deal more to the fine art of selling than telling a customer you will let him have one bottle of turpentine as a special favor, but he mustn't tell anybody. Those days are gone forever. Producers, processors and dealers of gum turpentine for too long have turned a deaf ear to threats of competition, real competition," the Association President asserted. "In the 1920's virtually every paint manufacturer in

the world used turpentine in the manufacture of ready mixed paints. Today, hardly a one does. They have shifted to mineral based solvents. We producers slept happily on while this happened to us. We produced the turpentine, shipped and forgot it. We hardly gave a thought to what it was going to be used for and we cared less," Langdale declared. "In the meantime, the production of wood and sulfate turpentine was increasing at a spectacular rate," he continued. " In 1933-34 there were 9,000 barrels of sulfate turps produced in the United States. In 1946-47, that production had risen to 120,000 barrels. Steam distilled turpentine during the period had risen from 83,000 barrels in 1933 to 175,000 barrels in 1946. Authoritative estimates for the season 1947-48 predict that gum turpentine will lag more than 10,000 barrels behind other types of turpentine," Langdale stated. "For the first time in the history of the United States, the gum industry stands as a minority producer of turpentine. For once we had been the one and only, we are now only one among others. The sale of gum turpentine for use as a paint thinner is the sole, the only, substantial market remaining for our product. The rest of them we have lost. If we lose this one then this is, as some of our gloomy prophets call it, a doomed industry. With an adequate advertising program we can sell turpentine," he asserted, "but we can do it if and only if we constantly and unremittingly hammer the message of turpentine's virtues into the householders of this nation. When such an advertising campaign is instituted and with the continued cooperation of the entire industry," the Association President concluded, "it would be impossible to defeat you. If they are not done, I can see no hope for the future."

AMERICAN TURPENTINE FARMERS ASSOCIATION
CO-OPERATIVE
ORGANIZATION OFFICES
VALDOSTA, GA.   TALLAHASSEE, FLA.

March 13, 1930

Wakulla Turpentine Co.,
Wakulla, Florida.

ORGANIZATION
COMMITTEE

L. M. AUTREY,
    CHAIRMAN.

R. E. McNEILL

W. P. SHELLEY

T. F. SMITH

E. P. ROSE

W. J. BOYNTON

J. B. DAVIS

A. V. KENNEDY

T. A. GRAHAM

H. LANGDALE

D. F. HOWELL

J. D. SELLERS

J. R. DASHER

W. L. FENDER

W. V. MUSGROVE

JIM BOWERS

MRS. W. P. SHELLEY,
    SECRETARY.

Dear Sir:

You have, of course, heard of the organization of this new Association, which is being supported by the leading producers throughout the entire turpentine belt.

I sent you under separate cover a copy of the By-laws and of the membership agreement, which I want you to look over very carefully indeed.

We believe that we have at last found a solution to many of the problems with which the Naval Stores industry has been faced.

We have been granted a Charter giving us exceptionally broad powers to solve these problems.

We have made wonderful progress, and we feel that the Association is deserving of the support of the entire naval stores industry. Without your support and the support of every other producer, its work will be hampered, but we cannot expect such support unless you are thoroughly familiar with the aims, purposes and policies of the Association and how it will affect us individually and as a body.

Therefore, at Mr. Shelly's suggestion, I am attending your meeting at Tallahassee on Thursday, March 20th, and I hope that you will not fail to be present.

With me will be Mr. Julian Langner, an expert in such organization work, and a nationally known authority on co-operative organization. Mr. Langner will explain very fully the basic plan of operation of this Association, and it will be well worth your while to be present that day, as you will find the information which will be given to you very interesting indeed.

I hope I may have the pleasure of meeting you personally at that time. In the meantime, I am,

Yours very truly,

L. M. Autrey

PRESIDENT.

A NON-PROFIT, NON-CAPITAL STOCK ASSOCIATION OF TURPENTINE FARMERS

NAVAL STORES *Review*

EST. 1890   WORLD-WIDE CIRCULATION

Published weekly by the H. L. Peace Publications, 433 West Church
St., Phone 5-5290, Jacksonville, Florida; Subscriptions $5.00 a year for
the United States and all foreign countries. Foreign air mail rates on
application. Single copies of weekly news edition 10c, monthly feature
edition 20c. Entered as a second class matter at the postoffice at Jacksonville, Florida, under the Act of March 3, 1879.

1978 Calendar of the American Turpentine
Farmers Association. The Association was
still in existence in 1978 but there is no
current listing of it in Valdosta today. (A)

The old country preacher rode up to the
house and said "Good Morning, Ma'am," in
a real polite-like way. "Is your husband at
home?" "Nope," said the old woman,
slamming her ax into the lighter knot so that
sparks flew, "he's off prowling around
somewhere in the woods, leaving me to do
the work." "Is he a God-fearing man?" the
preacher asked her. "I reckon he is, he totes
a rifle with him everywhere he goes so he
must be scared of something." "Ain't there
ever been any preachers around here?" the
preacher asked her. "Darned if I know,
Mister," she said, "look in the smokehouse,
if there's been ere one here, you'll find his
hide. He skins everything he kills."

When you find that a boil has commenced to
come on you, you rub the place with spirits
of turpentine and you will be surprised at
how quickly it will disappear.

Stop mice holes with old cloth saturated in
turpentine and the mice will not bother that
place anymore.

Rosin and turpentine barrels at the terminus
of the GF&A Railroad In Carrabelle, FL, mid
1930's. (FDS)

The Federal Naval Stores Act of 1923 was one of the most important laws passed relating to this industry. Among other accomplishments, this act prohibited interstate commerce of adulterated or mislabeled rosin and turpentine, set standards for the marketable products and provided for inspectors to check and mark (when requested) resin produced ready for sale and shipment. In 1934 the Agricultural Adjustment Administration made an agreement with the gum Naval Stores producers which restricted their production and prevented the industry from oversupplying a market already hit by the Depression. The Committee that was created provided a production quota for each state and a size (girth) limitation as to trees which could be worked. Operators were required to have licenses if operating under these provisions. The Commodities Credit Corporation (CCC) began making loans to turpentine farmers in 1934. The object of the CCC was the support of prices, which had dropped drastically when war began; however, the program was changed to encourage production of materials needed in the war effort. The Naval Stores Conservation Program was established under the Soil Conservation and Domestic Allotment Act of 1936. As part of this program the United States Forest Service sent men into the field to supervise the removal of turpentine faces from production as part of the crop reduction program. Research had shown that it was better not to work trees less than nine inches in diameter at chest level. Farmers were to be eligible for 25 cents a face for high cups and four cents a face for low cups less than 66 inches in height from the ground, from which cups had been removed by August 1, 1936. In 1940 the CCC loan program was not offered to anyone not participating in the conservation program. For 1941, the loan rate was 30 cents on a bulk gallon of turpentine, compared with 23 cents in 1940. For rosin, the loan rate was $1.95 for 100 lb. of Grade H.

In 1936, the American Turpentine Farmer's Association Cooperative (AT-FA) was organized and held its first meeting on July 8 at its headquarters in Valdosta, Georgia. A major force in keeping the industry solvent in time of need by providing loans and national advertising programs to boost sales, the AT-FA has acted as a lobby for the industry as well as obtaining research grants. As interest and support grew to help improve the turpentine industry during the 1930's various new methods were tried to increase production and centralize efforts. One new approach was chemical stimulation of the flow of gum or rosin. After many chemicals were tried, sulfuric acid was determined the most successful. The effective use of sulfuric acid came with the invention of a plastic spray gun in 1947, which began to be used by farmers shortly thereafter. The patent was awarded in 1950. By 1960, acid was believed to be used by about 90% of the industry's farmers. The use of acid reduced unnecessary cuts into trees and the worker needed only to strip off the bark. Better gutters were developed that avoided cutting into the tree to affix them and more of the tree was saved for lumber purposes, as well as increasing gum yield. At the experimental station in Olustee, they first developed a better fire distillation building and setting and better controls on the processes. Then came the invention and perfection of the batched steam distillation process, which was the first radical change in distillation methods in a century. This caused the stills to be more centralized since it was not practical to build a huge steam distillery on every turpentine farm. The batch steam distillation continued to have problems with the trash in the gum. The invention of the gum cleaning process in which the gum was filtered and washed first before being distilled caused any rosin product to be of higher quality. A later perfection was a change to the continuous steam distillation system which was not too different from batch distillation, except it saved labor, steam and floor space by running the still on a continuous basis. The new process reduced labor to almost zero. These improvements and changes, combined with better and more standardized marketing plans, revolutionized the industry. Some advantages of this new system were improvements in the quality of the final products, the control of the process, and the elimination of much waste associated with distillation. In the fire distillation process, quality depended on the local operator and his ability to run the still and to decide the input of water and so forth into the process. Control was virtually impossible, as witnessed by the method of running the still. Waste was at least 10% due to crude equipment and other factors. It should be mentioned that there had been developed by the early 1950's four ways of obtaining turpentine from rosin. The two major divisions were Gum Naval Stores, consisting of gum distillation by steam (formerly by fire), and Wood Naval Stores, consisting of the steam distillation of wood (that is pine stumps left from lumbering, destructive distillation of wood by heating pine wood, and sulfate pulping, creation of turpentine by the condensation of vapors which produced sulfate turpentine and tall oil). The products of these methods were called respectively, gum turpentine, steam distilled wood turpentine, destructively distilled wood turpentine and sulfate turpentine. The Naval Stores industry, thus, existed in two divisions after the advent of the research and new methods introduced since the 1930s.

The advent of strong competition with the production of turpentine by other means had caused great alarm within the Gum Naval Stores industry. Despite the inventions and other changes to the industry in the 20th Century, the industry had declined in the 30 years since World War II, mainly because of this rising competition and lack of innovation on its own behalf. In the face of this competition, two research studies done during these three decades indicated many of the problems suggested solutions in the form of recommendations and left many questions unanswered, the major one being "What is the future of the Gum Naval Stores industry?"

In 1971, the final report, entitled *A Study of the Problems and Potentials of the Gum Naval Stores Industry* was issued. The authors of this report emphasized the decline of the industry since 1950, pointed to the problems faced by the industry, and presented recommendations for change. One of the problems noted was the rise of competing industries, especially the tall oil industry, a byproduct of pulping, which was expected to exceed distilled rosin products in the early 1970's. The tall oil rosin was cheaper and had more stable prices than the gum distilled rosin. Another problem was concerned with final products. There had been no new developments of byproducts in gum distillation while replacements had arisen from new derivatives in the other branches of the industry to replace the older products. These other branch industries had arisen and could better fill the needs because of these new products developed through research. The Gum Naval Stores branch had sponsored very little research in the past 20 years and apparently none to help it compete with the new branch industries that had arisen in the meantime.

The final problem of the industry as a whole was the government price support system, which had been in effect since the 1930's. This did not help the Gum Naval Stores branch in competing with the other branches. Eighty percent of those surveyed felt it was essential to support the gum rosin farmers. The distilled gum products were kept in CCC stockpiles and this fact enforced insecurity when it came to prices since one was never sure when the CCC would release those stockpiles on the market.

There were also internal problems experienced by the industry that came to the surface during the surveys conducted with respect to the 1971 report. One major consideration was the total lack of innovation in gum gathering. They pointed to the wild forests, which were never planned, where gum gathering was very hard work and the same old method of chipping and dipping that had been used as long as anyone could recall was still being used. These operations had to be carried out on foot since the wild forest prevented any vehicles getting between the trees. Attempts to use mechanized equipment proved futile because of the excess weight of the mechanism and the distance between trees. Most of the cost attached to the final product was considered to be 60% labor. There was a severe shortage of workers due to low pay, low social status and low self-esteem, as well as the fact that the work was seasonal and usually took place far from any major city. There had been very little new labor secured by the industry and almost no recruitment program. Welfare programs were also cited as hindering employment and recruitment since it was felt the programs paid people not to work and often paid them more than the low wages of the Naval Stores industry.

One can tell by the decline in gum production from 1950 to 1960 that the industry was well on the way out. The number of crude gum producers in 1950 was 8,863. By 1960 there were only 1,222 left. The volume of crude gum produced in 1950 was 1,330,000 barrels. In 1960, only 194,635 barrels were produced. The estimated number of workers in 1950 was 21,000. By 1960 it was down to 3,300. The course of continually decreasing production in the face of a diminishing supply of labor and decreasing acreage under production can lead to but one end, and that is the death of an industry that once stood tall among all others in the Southeast. This does not have to happen, indeed it is inconceivable that it should.

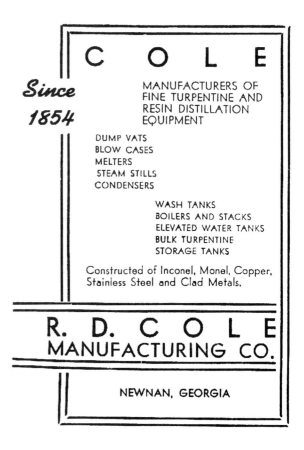

HARRY LEE BAKER
STATE FORESTER
H. A. SMITH
ASST. STATE FORESTER

STATE BOARD OF FORESTRY

S. BRYAN JENNINGS, PRESIDENT
N. J. WICKER, VICE PRESIDENT
SIMON F. WILLIAMS, SECY.
J. B. GLEN
A. A. PAYNE

Florida Forest Service

RENDERING ASSISTANCE
TO THE LANDOWNERS AND FOREST INDUSTRIES
IN APPLIED FORESTRY AND FOREST PROTECTION

Tallahassee, Fla.
May 1st
1930

Dear Friend of The Forest:

A phonograph record "De Woods of Pine", a darky song that tells in a beautiful and convincing manner that "De Wolf am coming right in de door, when de old Piney Woods ain't here no more", may be obtained from the Florida Forest Service, Tallahassee, Florida, for 75¢, no charge for shipping carton and postage; provided, orders are placed for at least fifty records.

You will enjoy listening to this phonograph record because it carries a real message on fire prevention and timber growing. You will enjoy it because the song is most pleasing and as good as many you find on the open market. You may want to use this method of reaching your friends with a forest conservation message.

The words of the song are found on the reverse side of this sheet.

Please draw your check in favor of the Florida Forest Service for 75¢. If fifty such checks are not received, yours will be returned.

This call is going out to 1,000 "Friends of the Forest". We ought to put this over and reach thousands with our message.

Your cooperation will be very much appreciated.

Very sincerely yours,

HLB/S

Harry Lee Baker
State Forester

Forest Fires Make
**Idle Lands
Idle Industries
Idle Hands**
Stop Fires, Grow Trees
Keep Forest Land Working

Dedicated to Pine Institute of America

DE WOODS OF PINE

Poem by
Warren Nicke

Music by
Lucille DeMert

(1)

An old darky singin' in de woods of pine
 A workin de trees for turpentine,
My luck hit grows with the Piney Wood
 And while pines grow my luck stays good
Food in de kitchen and de times ain't hard
 When a man works out in God's front yard.

Chorus

Pay day's comin' while de pine trees grow,
 Hits de surest thing dat a man can know
De wolf am a coming right in de door,
 When de old Piney Wood ain't here no more

(2)

Listen honey if you want to farm
 Don't let de Piney Wood come to harm
Dey's always workin for de farmer hard
 Like great big soldier men a standin' guard
Keepin' way drought de frost de bugs
 Oh happy am de farm de Piney Woods hugs

(3)

When you hear de wind a hummin in de pine
 Hit makes a tune dat sounds mighty fine
De big pine trees are a makin dat sound
 A talkin' to dere babies close to de ground
Little pine babies growin' down below
 Gotta help dem babies if dey's goin' to grow

(4)

When you hear de big old pine trees start to moan
 Dere's fire in de woods dat makes dem groan
De little fire kills de little baby trees
 De grass and birds, but no ticks nor fleas
Big fires kill de big trees too,
 We gotta stop de fires whatever we do.

16

Then — SUDS FOR SLIPPER BATHERS

Now — TOUGHENER FOR RUBBER

When slipper tubs were in vogue, fashionable ladies often used a greaseless soap made from rosin. (Illustration courtesy of The Bettmann Archive.)

ANOTHER DEVELOPMENT IN NAVAL STORES MADE POSSIBLE THROUGH HERCULES CHEMICAL RESEARCH

Since the advent of naval stores, rosin has been used in toilet and laundry soap. Now, through Hercules research, there is a new and entirely different type of "soap." Known as Dresinate* 731, it serves as the emulsifier and toughener in the GR-S-10-type rubbers for today's longer-wearing, cooler-running tires.

Through constant research in rosin and terpene chemistry, Hercules has developed many other important aids to industry. Each of them has resulted in greater demand for products of the Southern Pine, and has helped make Hercules Powder Company the world's largest buyer and consumer of rosin.

HERCULES POWDER COMPANY

989 MARKET STREET, WILMINGTON 99, DELAWARE

*REG. U. S. PAT. OFF. BY HERCULES POWDER COMPANY

NAVAL STORES MARKETING CORPORATION

CODES USED:
ACME
BENTLEY'S COMPLETE PHRASE

JACKSONVILLE, FLA.   SAVANNAH, GA.

CABLE ADDRESS
"NAMARK"

SAVANNAH, GA.

May 9, 1930.

Gentlemen:-

At the request of a number of operators, we together
with a majority of the factors, are calling a meeting of the
Naval Stores Producers, one at Jacksonville on Wednesday, May,
14th at 1:30 P. M., Jacksonville Chamber of Commerce, and one at
Savannah on Thursday, May 15th, at 1:30 P. M., at Savannah Morning
News Town Hall, corner of Bay and Whitaker Streets, to consider
the present emergency in the Naval Stores Trade, and to take steps,
if possible, to prevent worse conditions and to re-establish a
normal basis.

As we are all aware, business conditions all over the
world are upset, with a lessening of demand, and the price of
commodities falling all along the line. Naval Stores, from a
price standpoint, has been one of the commodities to suffer the
most, and unless some action is taken we may see further declines,
and perhaps a tie-up, where the producer and factor will have to
carry the goods until trade is re-established. The situation
with reference to our products is aggravated by what we believe
to be the lack of sufficient funds in the distributing end of the
business. It requires a large capital to finance the marketing
of the crops, as all of the offerings at the ports have to be
bought, and the stocks on hand carried, or otherwise we have no
market. The producing end of the business has many millions of
dollars involved, while the total capital invested in the marketing end amounts to very little in proportion. This is a situation
that must be corrected if we are to hope for any improvement.

We urge you to forego any other demands upon your time,
and not fail to attend one or the other of these meetings, as any
results attained will depend upon the response of the operator.
If we act together in unity, we feel certain that great benefits
can be obtained; but it is not possible to do anything unless it
is practically unanimous, and unless these meetings are fully
attended, and everyone does his part, nothing can be done, and
there is no telling what the end will be.

We trust you will give this letter your serious consideration and do everything possible to attend the meeting.

Yours very truly,

NAVAL STORES MARKETING CORP.

December 13, 1930.

Gentlemen:-

During the month of December, each year, more dross is shipped than during any other two or three months of the year, due to the fact that most operators ship their dross after they wind up all woods operations.

Because of the heavy receipts just at this time and the fact that we always make it a rule to remit promptly for all dross the same day the shipments reach us, we find it necessary to withdraw our road men between now and January 1st, as we need their assistance in helping us to quickly weigh up and remit for dross arriving at our plant.

While our men will not be able to call on you at your place again during December and, even though we may have to reduce our price if the rosin market does not show some improvement by January 1st, you need not hesitate to ship your dross on to us, as we will protect our present price on any dross that shows Bill of Lading dating in December.

Our present price is $14.00 per ton for Batting Dross and $9.00 per ton for Strainer dross, if separated; $14.00 per ton for Batting and $7.00 per ton for Strainer Dross, if mixed, all fob cars Jacksonville.

We will remit promptly upon receipt of all shipments, and, in the meantime should you want any further information in regard to your dross please call us over the telephone collect, or wire us collect. Our telephone number is 5-1410 Jacksonville, call us at our expense and we will appreciate it.

Respectfully,

PAPER MAKERS CHEMICAL CORPORATION.

Things that come to Mind	Fried Fish
Old cowboy never drinks downstream from the herd and he don't squat to go with his spurs on.	Take a mixture of corn meal, salt and pepper, bread your fish in the mixture and drop them into hot hog lard and fry them until golden brown.

19

Dear Sir;-

On next Thursday, April 17th. we shall hold our regular monthly meeting in Tallahassee at the Elk's Club at one o'clock Eastern time. Officers will be elected and plans worked out for this year.

For three years this association has held its regular meetings. A remarkable feeling of good fellowship has grown up among its members. Many Speakers of note, experts in their lines, have addressed us. Local problems of operators have been discussed and in some measure solved as a result of the round table discussion: which are an important part of every program. Much that we as an Association can accomplish remains to be done.

COME to this meeting Thursday. Let's elect the right officers, plan the right program and make this the biggest, best year we have ever had.

Yours truly,

MIDDLE FLORIDA TURPENTINE PRODUCERS ASSOCIATION.

By *W. P. Shelly*
Secretary-Treasuer.

A typical old bursting turpentine man had, by some means, gotten into heaven and was bragging about Niagara Falls and how big it was. An old shriveled up woman near him started to giggle and laugh. "Do you mean to say," said the turpentine hand, "that you think 8 million cubic feet of water each minute is not a lot of water? Might I ask what your name is?" "Certainly," replied the woman, "I'm Mrs. Noah."

For burns, take equal parts of rosin, mutton tallow or pure lard. Melt together and put in a container, glass or earthenware, that may be closed up tight. If Poppy buds or flowers can be procured, fry them first and strain them, then add the rosin and so forth. This eases the burn and it will never blister if used at once.

Carson Naval Stores Company,

LIBERTY BANK & TRUST CO. BUILDING

WAREHOUSE
303 RIVER ST. EAST

SAVANNAH. GEORGIA,

BRANCH OFFICE:
JACKSONVILLE. FLA.

September 26th. 1930'

For Your Serious Consideration.

No definite upward trend has as yet developed in the general business situation. Occasional improvements are noted but these are "spotty". Commodity prices continue at levels unprofitable to producers and there is widespread unemployment both in this and foreign contries. Unemployment leads to unrest and already there have been political revolutions in Germany and several South American countries and others may follow. India and China are seething with rebellion. Disturbed conditions injure the normal flow of business and all industries, including our own, are affected adversely. Where countries are torn with internal strife their purchasing power is reduced sharply. When a laborer is out of a job or a farmer or merchant is carrying on an unprofitable business he defers painting his house and barn and there is less turpentine consumed. Decrease in production is necessary in order to balance the supply with the demand. Operators and factors should give their best efforts to this end otherwise another year of low prices will follow. Do not expect the other fellow to cut his production while reserving the right unto yourself to maintain yours, but join wholeheartedly and sincerely in the movement to place the naval stores producing industry upon a sound and paying basis and start planning now accordingly.

Yours very truly,

CARSON NAVAL STORES COMPANY.

Tea

Place a cup full of tea in a gallon sized jug with an open top in the early morning. Cover it with just a little bit of cold spring water. When you get ready to serve it, put it in a pitcher and pour full of water. This should make a gallon.

Grape Juice made from Wild Muscadines

Gather the grapes in late July or early August, when they are fully ripe. Take the stems off them and wash well. Place in a large pot, cover with water, and boil until they are well done. Strain the juice through a piece of muslin, pour into jars and seal while it is still hot.

Hon. --------
U. S. Senate,
Washington, D. C.

Dear Senator -------:

The amendments proposing to put a forty-five per cent (45%) duty on china wood oil (tung oil), palm oil, palm kernel oil, and inedible olive oils will, without question, seriously curtail the domestic consumption of rosin by the varnish and soap maker. As these two industries represent over fifty per cent of the domestic consumption of rosin any such decrease will be disastrous to the naval stores industry. The market price for our product has been for several years below the cost of production.

There are approximately fifteen hundred producers of naval stores, besides an unknown large number of people who produce only the crude gum. Furthermore, every man who has any pine timber land, no matter how small the acreage, has a direct interest. It has been estimated that approximately five hundred thousand people throughout the naval stores belt will be affected.

I sincerely believe that the proposed duty will be decidely harmful to the naval stores industry without any compensating recompense to any one else. I, therefore, respectfully urge you to aggressively oppose the proposed duty and protect the naval stores industry.

Respectfully,

SAVANNAH, GEORGIA, NAVAL STORES MARKET
REPORTS OF SAVANNAH COTTON AND NAVAL STORES EXCHANGE, WEEK ENDING APRIL 24, 1947
SPIRITS TURPENTINE — BULK PRICES (In Gallons)

Day	Friday April 18	Saturday April 19	Monday April 21	Tuesday April 22	Wednesday April 23	Thursday April 24
Price	$0.85	No Trading	$0.86	$0.86	$0.86	$0.85
Sales, Gallons	7,400	—	24,000	—		16,350
Offerings, Gallons	23,400	—	24,000	—	—	16,350
Receipts, Gallons	12,800	—	12,350	16,150	—	8,300

ROSIN (Quotations per 100 lbs. net — In Drums)

Day	April 18	April 19	April 21	April 22	April 23	April 24
X	9 75	No Trading	9 75	9 50	9 25	9 25
WW	9 75	—	9 75	9 50	9 25	9 25
WG	9 25	—	9 25	9 25	9 25	9 15
N	9 25	—	9 25	9 25	9 25	9 04
M	9 10	—	9 10	9 10	9 10	9 00
K	9 10	—	9 10	9 10	9 10	8 90
I	9 00	—	9 00	9 00	9 00	8 90
H	9 00	—	9 00	9 00	9 00	8 90
G	9 00	—	9 00	9 00	9 00	8 90
F	8 90	—	8 90	8 90	8 90	8 80
E	8 75	—	8 75	8 75	8 75	8 75
D	8 00	—	8 00	8 00	8 00	8 00
B	8 00	—	8 00	8 00	8 00	8 00
Sales Drums	100	—	15	3 59	248	426
Offerings, Drums	100	—	15	3 59	490	426
Receipts, Drums	13	27	—	76	47	305

FOREST PLANTING IN FLORIDA
480,000 PINE TREES WILL BE PLANTED

"I'se worked in turpentine all my life, but never set out pine trees before". These words are heard as the Florida Forest Service men supervise the planting of one year old pines.

With only 6,000 trees set out last year the interest in forest tree planting has increased tremendously as nearly one-half a million will go in the ground this season. The majority of these are from the Florida Forest Service Nursery maintained at the State Farm at Raiford, Florida. About 310,000 slash and longleaf are being sold at $4.00 per thousand to land owners who wish to make their idle acres productive. Private seed beds or nurseries supervised by the Forest Service have an output of 170,000. These sturdy young pines are from seed or "pine mass" planted last January.

These pines are furnished by the Forest Service at cost of $4.00 per thousand. This number will plant from 1-1/3 to 3-1/3 acres, depending on the spacing used. The labor charge covering the planting of these trees is about equal to the cost of the trees as two common laborers can easily plant over 1,000 pines in a day. No watering or fertilizing is necessary, the only care being protection from fire. This is especially essential in the early life of these trees. Last year a survival of 85% resulted from the plantings which is very satisfactory. Ordinarily a 75% survival is considered a success according to Mr. C. H. Coulter, Forest Assistant, who is in charge of this work.

Over 100 separate plantings will be made this season, forty-five of which will be demonstration plots located adjacent to well traveled county roads or State Highways. The plans for next year call for doubling the capacity of the State Nursery to supply the increased demand.

C. 1947

NAVAL STORES *Review*

EST. 1890

WORLD-WIDE CIRCULATION

Published weekly by the H. L. Peace Publications, 433 West Church St., Phone 5-5290, Jacksonville, Florida; Subscriptions $5.00 a year for the United States and all foreign countries. Foreign air mail rates on application. Single copies of weekly news edition 10c, monthly feature edition 20c. Entered as a second class matter at the postoffice at Jacksonville, Florida under the Act of March 3, 1879.

"Good heavens, who gave you that black eye?" " A bridegroom, for kissing the bride after the wedding." " But, surely he didn't object to that ancient custom?" " No, but it was two years after the ceremony."

For boils, take peach tree leaves, chop them up fine. Boil in water. Thicken it with flour. Put in a few drops of turpentine. Make a poultice and put on the boil while it is warm.

Beef Tea

To one pound of lean beef add one and a half tumblers of cold water. Cut the beef into small pieces. Cover and let it boil slowly for 10 minutes. Add a little salt after it is boiled.

Bannocks

Use one pint of cornmeal. Pour on it boiling water to thoroughly wet it. Let it stand a few minutes. Add salt, one egg and a little sweet cream or a tablespoon of melted butter. Make it into balls and fry in hot lard.

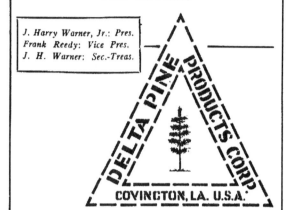

The doctor was called on the telephone by an old woman that used to work for his wife. In great agitation, the woman told the doctor that her youngest child was in a bad way. "What seems to be the trouble?" "Nothing seems to be the trouble, doc, only the baby got a fit and a spasm, like she's gonna die right off." "Well, what did you imagine? Have you any idea as to the cause?" "I ain't got no idea, doc, unless it was a bottle of ink she done swallowed this afternoon." "I'll be right over to see her," said the doctor quickly, "have you done anything for her." "Well, doctor, I made her swallow three pieces of ink blotter paper. That was all she could get down."

Coffee

Coffee is a tonic and stimulating beverage. For eight cups, use nearly eight cups of water. Put in coffee, as much as you like. Boil a minute and take off and throw in a cup of cold water to sink the grounds to the bottom. In five minutes, it will be very clear. Or beat one or two eggs, which mix with ground coffee to form a ball. Nearly fill bucket with cold water, simmer gently for half an hour, having introduced the ball. Do not boil or you will destroy the aroma. Coffee made this way is best cooked over an open fire in a gallon sized metal syrup bucket. Fresh spring water is best.

WOODS

In the research of current day writings about the turpentine industry, I find references made to imply that the woods rider "sported a pistol and whip" to keep the hands under control. I can personally state without hesitation, having been raised with the woods riders and the hands and lived with them for about 40 years of my life, I never saw a woods rider with a whip. The only ones I saw with a pistol didn't "sport" it, they carried it in their pocket usually, and it was not for controlling the hands, it was for killing snakes. Another misconception that I've found is that the hands were not allowed outside the turpentine camp area, that they were restricted to the camp or woods work areas. Some writers go so far as to say that leaving the camp was forbidden. During my time with the people of that era and industry, I have known the hands to walk through the woods on weekends, going from camp to camp. One could almost know which hand was passing because he was singing his favorite song or hollering his favorite holler, the same holler he would use in the woods to let the tally man know that he had completed his assigned work. They were a happy people and sang almost all the time. Many of the hands hunted or trapped and I would often see them working their trap lines. They had free access to fishing the rivers, sinkholes and streams around the area of the camp that were within walking distance and they seemed to get an immense enjoyment out of catfishing, which was one of their favorite pastimes. They were also noted for going through the woods picking berries, persimmon, nuts, any edible wild plants or foods that they could find during season.

Dedicated to Pine Institute of America

DE WOODS OF PINE

Poem By   Music By
Warren Nicke   Lucille DeMert

(1)
An old darky singin' in de woods of pine
A workin de trees for turpentine,
My luck hit grows with the Piney Wood
And while pines grow my luck stays good
Food in de kitchen and de times ain't hard
When a man works out in God's front yard.

Chorus
Pay day's comin' while de pine trees grow,
Hits de surest thing dat a man can know
De wolf am a coming right in de door,
When de old Piney Wood ain't here no more

(2)
Listen honey if you want to farm
Don't let de Piney Wood come to harm
Dey's always workin for de farmer hard
Like great big soldier men a standin' guard
Keepin' way drought de frost de bugs
Oh happy am de farm de Piney Woods hugs

(3)
When you hear de wind a hummin in de pine
Hit makes a tune dat sounds mighty fine
De big pine trees are a makin dat sound
A talkin' to dere babies close to de ground
Little pine babies growin' down below
Gotta help dem babies if dey's goin' to grow

(4)
When you hear de big old pine trees start to moan
Dere's fire in de woods dat makes dem groan

De little fire kills de little baby trees
De grass and birds, but no ticks nor fleas
Big fires kill de big trees too,
We gotta stop de fires whatever we do.

(Words to a phonograph record offered by the Florida Forest Service in a letter dated May 1, 1930.)

There was a period of time between 1875 and 1923 that turpentine and logging operators were allowed to lease prisoners from the states. These prisoners were housed in the woods in "stockades" and kept under guard. Records indicate that about 30% of the leased prisoners would escape each year so the operators were required not only to keep them under guard, but to have trained dogs to track them down if necessary.

The practice of cutting a gum cavity (box) in the base of the tree to collect gum was called boxing the tree. Collecting the gum at the base of the tree began in about 1700 and continued until the invention and use of the Herty cup in 1902. The collection of raw gum for distilling became an important part of the Naval Stores industry after the invention of the copper fire still in 1834. (A)

This boxed tree located on McBride Slough in Wakulla County, FL was worked to a height of 16 feet. (A)

The use of the cup and gutter system in turpentining was credited to Dr. Charles H. Herty (1867-1938). Herty, a chemist at the University of Georgia, was on a sabbatical to Europe when he heard a German professor relate how the Americans butchered the pine trees by cutting a box into the tree to collect the resin and sometimes ruined future growth of the tree. Herty was also able to see cups, a new innovation, being used to collect gum in France at this time. He returned to Georgia late in the summer of 1900 and started a crusade to better the turpentine industry with an initial visit to Valdosta in October of that year. On October 31, he sent a questionnaire to many boards of trade and chambers of commerce throughout the South in an attempt to learn more about the turpentine industry. Judging from the replies he received, this was not an extremely helpful venture. Herty's letter to the United States Department of Agriculture-Forest Service Bureau in Washington produced better results. After he invented the clay, or Herty, turpentine cup to replace the box method of collecting gum he was hired by the Forest Service first as a collaborator at $300 a year and later as an expert at $ 2000 a year. The Forest Service sponsored his experiments at Ocilla, Georgia in 1902, the results of which proved that the cup and gutter system of collecting gum or resin was far superior to the old box method. Herty applied for a patent for an apparatus for collecting crude turpentine on August 16, 1902 and received it the following year. His results at Ocilla were published in the Bureau of Forestry Bulletin, # 40 in 1903, entitled *A New Method of Turpentine Orcharding*. Herty then assumed the role of major proponent for his new cup and gutter method and went on a lecture circuit to convince farmers to change to this method of gum collecting in which his cup was the main innovation. He often spoke at county courthouses with evangelistic fervor. Herty also initiated the production of a cup which was first manufactured in Daisy, Tennessee.

If a cup was to be placed on the same tree the next year, it was taken off and turned upside down at the base of the tree or hung upside down on the nail in the face. This was to keep the rain from collecting in the cup and the water freezing during cold weather, which would break the clay cups or crack the metal cups at the seams. In the early part of the 20th Century, the Herty cup was the most common style on the market. Established in 1902, Herty Turpentine Company produced at least 60,000 cups per day until about 1914, when the advent of the galvanized tin cup caused a decrease in the demand for clay cups. These cups were marketed throughout the industry. A clay cup, shaped to fit the tree was produced and marketed during the first quarter of the 20th Century. As early as 1914, galvanized tin cups were on the market. Styles included the flower pot shaped "birdseye cup", the trapezoid shaped "buzzard wing" cup and a variety of metal oblong cups. During the 1920s and 30s, there were several different styles of galvanized tin cups being manufactured and marketed. The aluminum cup came into wide use in the late 1940's.

Old Abe owned a well-known racehorse for which Ike offered him ten thousand dollars. Abe accepted the offer and a check, promising to send the horse on the next day. Overnight, the horse died, but Abe could not bear to lose his bargain, so he cashed the check and sent the horse on. He heard nothing further and did his best to avoid Ike. Unfortunately, the day came when they met face to face. Abe took the bull by the horns and asked Ike what had become of the horse. "Well," said Ike, "when I found it was dead, seeing that everyone knew what a wonderful horse it was, I raffled it off and 25 people bought tickets at $500 each." "But," said Abe, "didn't anyone grumble?" "Only the man that won it," replied Ike, "and I gave him his money back."

General directions for making Bread

In the composition of good bread, there are three important requisites - good flour, good yeast, and strength to knead it well. Flour should be white and dry, crumbling easily again after it is pressed in by hand. A very good method of ascertaining the quality of yeast will be to add a little flour to a very small quantity, setting it in a warm place. If, in the course of 10 or 15 minutes, it rises, it will do to use. When you make bread, first set the sponge with warm milk or water, keeping it in a warm place until quite light, then mold the sponge by adding flour into one large loaf, kneading it well. Set this to rise again and then when sufficiently light, mold it into smaller loaves. Let it rise again, then bake it. Care should be taken not to get the dough too stiff with flour. It should be as soft as it can be to knead it well. To make bread or biscuits a nice color, wet the dough over the top with water just before putting it into the oven. Flour should always be sifted.

The heart of two trees from the early metal cup years. Both of these trees were about three times as big as shown before the sapwood rotted off. (A)

Harvesting the old stumps and fat light wood. This fat light wood was shipped to Hercules Powder Co. in Brunswick, GA where the resin was cooked out of it. In 1850 twenty percent of the Naval Stores produced were extracted from dead heart pine trees, stumps and knots. (A)

January 30th,1932.

Consolidated Naval Stores Company,

Jacksonville,Florida.

Dear Sirs.-

     Please order for us 2 Crops of the Hert Clay Cups,

to be shipped to Wakulla,Florida, Prepay Station S.A.L.Ry.

     Also about 6000 Lbs 2" galv gutter strips, these we will

probably houl from Jacksonville.

               Yours truly,

               WAKULLA TURPENTINE COMPANY.

        By

               Sec & Tres.

The city boys wanted to grow up to be firemen, ride on a big red fire truck and fight fires. The boy that lived near the railroad yards wanted to grow up to be an engineer, drive the train and carry freight back and forth from one place to another. The boy in the turpentine woods wanted to grow up to be a tally man, ride a pretty horse and have a big tallywacker.

Hot Chocolate

To each quart of new milk, allow three heaping tablespoons full of straight chocolate. It is best to set your gallon syrup bucket that you are going to cook it in a kettle of boiling water. Pour in the milk and, as it heats, add the chocolate mix to a paste with a little milk. Boil for two or three minutes and serve. Some prefer to boil chocolate only one minute, others fifteen. Set aside to cool a little so that the oil may be removed and then reheat when wanted.

There was an old woods rider that worked in our area in the turpentine woods. He owned a Model A Ford and was accused of being so tight that he wouldn't look through the windshield of the car, he'd stick his head out the window when he drove, he was afraid he'd wear the windshield out. When he'd find him a girlfriend and think about getting married, he would go home and set two plates on the table. He would eat the food out of one plate and throw the other away, just to see how much it would cost him to feed two people, then make the decision that he wasn't ready to pay the price of feeding another mouth. They say he was so tight that when he blinked his eyes, his naval would wink.

The woods were divided into drifts and crops for working purposes. Sign on a pine tree indicating the drift and crop number. D is for drift and 1 A is the drift number. The 11-40 is the crop number. A drift was 1,000 trees and a crop was 10,000 trees. The average drift was about 40 acres with the size varying according to the density of the trees. Hands would be assigned to work within a drift each day. Along with the hands was a tally man who carried a tally board and a stick. The stick (called a tallywacker) could have been a walking stick, billy club or anything of that type. Each hand had a different way of communicating with the tally man. He would sing out his holler when he finished a tree and the tally man would recognize him and put a mark on the tally board by his name so he could get paid properly for his work. If the tally man saw a tree that hadn't been raked around, chipped, dipped or scraped properly, he would hit the tree with his tallywacker and the hand that had worked that tree would know to come back and redo his job. The tally man's duties were to supervise the work in the woods and make sure it was done properly. The bigger operations had a woods rider who was a step above the tally man and one position below the owner of the turpentine operation. (A)

31

Recommended Naval Stores Practices
1937

The following Naval Stores practices and specifications were prepared by state and federal Naval Stores experts and were approved by the Southeastern Section of the Society of American Foresters:

I.   Tree Selection

   A. Use a 9 inch minimum diameter limit. There may be a latitude of 1" depending on growth rate of trees. A good 8" slash runs 40 barrels. A poor 9.5" longleaf runs only 35 barrels.
   B. Eliminate poor trees such as spiked topped, badly leaning and suppressed trees with less than 25% crown length

II.   Hanging Cups

   A. Use rustless or rust-free cups, gutters and aprons.
   B. Scribe face width at 1/3 breast height circumference or 12" maximum.
   C. Expose little or no wood below the gutters and aprons.
   D. Set the cups level.
   E. Restrict incisions for the gutters and aprons not to exceed the depth of the streak.
   F. Install cups as low as practicable.
   G. Hogals are helpful in preventing heavy slabbing for seating cups.
   H. Gutter chisels or broadaxes and mauls maintain control over the depth of incisions for gutters and aprons better than free hand broad ax strokes.
   I. The pitch of the gutters should be sufficient to keep the gum from clogging.

III. Working trees

   A. Height of face shall be from 14" to 16" each season.
   B. Depth of streak shall be 5/8" for slash or 3/4" for longleaf. Very thrifty timber may be worked deeper for limited periods, but chipping for old or closely grown timber should be 1/2"
   C. The peak angle shall be 130 degrees for the first three years, not sharper than 90 degrees thereafter.
   D. In the absence of definite knowledge, a square streak is recommended.
   E. Cut streaks weekly.
   F. Double streaking is permissible in June, July and August.
   G. Maintain shoulders at the same level.
   H. Keep chipping tools sharp and well cut (honed) out.
   I. Use a chip paddle which covers tins and cups.
   J. Cut an advance streak if possible during November and December, not later than February 1.
   K. Keep shoulder lines straight.

IV.   Back faces

   A. Two faces shall not be worked concurrently except when early cutting is planned.
   B. If a third face is desired, place a second face only when a 4"and a 10" bar can be maintained.
   C. At least 4" bars shall be maintained between faces.
   D. The rest period depends upon growth, number of faces planned and final size of tree desired when the last face is worked out. Ordinarily this will be from four to ten years if three faces are desired and a 16" tree is wanted after it is worked out for turpentine.

V.   Raising

   A.   Raise preferably yearly depending
        upon economic conditions.
   B.   Tack in streaks or
   C.   Restrict incisions to 1/4" radial depth
        or
   D.   Drive tins in jump peaks.

VI.   Supervision

   A.   Close supervision for best work is
        essential.
   B.   Inspect periodically and rate the
        work of woods riders for
        comparison.
   C.   Keep records of production and cost
        per crop.

VII.   Scraping

   A.   Avoid slabbing wood from faces.
   B.   Punching scrape at each dipping is
        good practice.
   C.   Use winged scrape box for low faces
        and push-up bucket for high faces.

VIII.   Dipping

   A.   Dip at least every four streaks.
   B.   Where possible, dip on two streaks.
   C.   A wood dip paddle is recommended
        for zinc, aluminum and painted cups.

A face prepared at the base of a tree in January and February. The bulk of the turpentine and rosin came from the longleaf and slash pines in the southeastern United States. (A)

Sassafras Tea

In the Spring, gather small roots and tender twigs from the Sassafras tree. Pound the roots to a pulp if they are very big and wash them, along with the twigs. Boil them, strain the juice and then sweeten it to your taste.

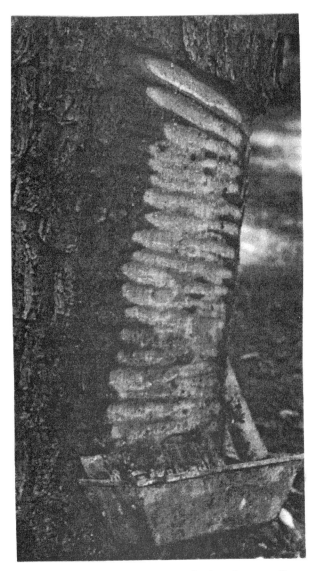

New face, cup, apron and gutter, with the first streak in place. In March the hands began their rounds every week making a streak on each tree. (A)

The cup, gutter, apron and streaks on the tree. From the scar in the tree the gum oozed out and ran down the face into the cup. Once a week for about 36 weeks each year the hand made a new cut in the bark. Each cut was just above that of the previous week. By the end of the first season, early in November, there was a face on the side of the tree, varying from ten inches to 15 inches in width according to the size of the tree and would be about 16 inches in height. The face would be extended during the following years to a height of eight to ten feet. (A)

Biscuits

Mix and pour the sweet milk with 1/2 cup of melted butter. Stir in a pinch of salt, 2 teaspoons of baking powder and flour enough for a stiff batter. Get the oven good and hot, probably around 400 degrees. Drop the batter a spoonful at a time into a pan of flour. Roll them in the flour getting it over all of the outside. Put them in a buttered skillet. Press your knuckles into each biscuit, making an indentation enough to hold a 1/2 teaspoon of melted butter. Add the butter, then bake about 15 minutes in the oven.

Fried Mush

When desired to be fried for breakfast, turn into an earthen dish and set away to cool, then cut in slices when you wish to fry. Dip each piece into beaten eggs and fry on a hot griddle greased with hog lard.

Liniment to rub onto areas that ache. 1 cup of turpentine. 1 cup of vinegar. 1 egg. Mix it all together and shake well.

Cup, with cup cover, using the hack to make the streak on the tree. A good hand could work as many as 1500 faces in a day depending on how dense the trees were. Chipping took a few strokes to make the cut in the bark. (USDA)

Stewed Figs

Take four ounces of fine sugar, the thin rind of a large lemon and a pint of cold water. When the sugar is dissolved, add one pound of turkey figs and place stew pan over a moderate fire so they may heat and swell slowly and stew gently for two hours. When they are quite tender, add the juice of one lemon, arrange them in a glass dish and serve cold.

Syrup Cookies

3 cups syrup
1 heaping tsp soda
1 cup butter
1 Tbs. ginger
1/2 cup hog lard
1 cup hot water

Roll thick and bake in a moderate oven. It is better if left standing awhile.

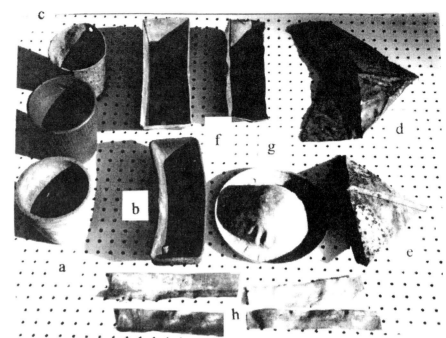

a. Two Herty type cups patented August 16, 1902 and used in the industry until the 1930's. It was hung on a nail at the bottom of the face with two gutters to direct the gum into it. b. Clay cup that was made later (probably about 1915) in a curved shape so it would better fit the tree. c. "Birdseye" metal cup made and used in the same way as the clay Herty cup. d and e "buzzard wing" cups. d was nailed directly to the tree and didn't require an apron or gutter. It did not prove very successful. e used with a gutter and was hung on a nail in the tree. f. After 1915, cups made of galvanized tin or aluminum were used. The lip of the cup was hung under the apron with the cup supported on a nail. Galvanized cups that were damaged by fire would rust. The zinc used to coat the tin to make it rustless was melted when a cup was heated by fire. Aluminum cups, which would not rust, came into wide use after the 2nd World War. g. An experimental cup. I have excavated three of these in my explorations around turpentine camps, but I don't understand how they were used. h. Two aprons and two gutters. The aprons and gutters, which were pieces of galvanized tin, were placed on the trees to direct the flow of gum into the cup. It was very important that a type of material that would not rust be used. Rust discolored the gum and caused the rosin produced from it to have a darker color, which decreased its market value. (A)

Light wood knots from virgin pines. Knots from today's tree are only about two inches around and three or four inches long. These knots were from trees that were twice the size of the length of the knot, which would make the tree no less than six feet in diameter. (A)

36

Dipping the gum. About every third week, as judged by the woods rider, a crew made the rounds gathering the raw gum from the cups and putting it into barrels for hauling to the turpentine still. (A)

Turpentine lease. It was a common practice to lease timber for turpentining. According to a survey made by the United States Forest Service, 73% of the turpentine crops during the 1934-35 season were leased by processors. Owners leased timber for turpentining at so much per face, or cup. The price varied. It depended on a number of factors, such as the price of turpentine and rosin, the distance from a shipping point, the size and quantity of trees and the cost of labor. In 1926 it was not uncommon for owners to receive 7 cents per face per year. In 1937, after the Depression, the price was lower. Lease prices for that year ranged from 4 to 5 cents per face per year. Some timberland owners preferred to make leases on a percentage basis. When this was done, the owner received a percentage of the gross sale value of the turpentine and rosin produced. It was generally recognized that better conservation practices would be used if all timber was worked by owners. A timberland owner was naturally more interested in using practices to conserve his timber than would the average person to whom he might lease. If timber was leased it was using good business judgment to have a written contract. The terms of the lease would be such as to prevent the exploitation of timber, but would not impose undue hardship on the operator. Some landowners worked their own timber and either sold the gum to a nearby processor or arranged for it to be stilled on a commission basis. The practice was usually much more profitable than leasing, especially for owners of small timber tracts. Turpentine operators did not like to lease small lots of timber and often would pay a lower price per face if leased. With small tracts a number of leases would be made and often land lines would have to be surveyed in order to establish correct ownership, which required time and was expensive. There was a trend by more and more owners to work their own timber and sell the raw gum to processors with large, well equipped centralized stills. Some small operators found they could make more by selling raw gum than by processing it for marketing the rosin and turpentine. Farmers with small tracts of longleaf and slash pine could usually use their own farm labor for working the trees.

G. A. Gerrell

To

Chason & Register

TURPENTINE LEASE
DATED: December 18, 1926
CONSIDERATION: $53.00
GRANTING: Grant, bargain, lease & convey
HABENDUM: Their heirs and assigns
WARRANTY: See below
RECORDED: December 27, 1926
DEED BOOK 14, Page 563

* * * lease and convey unto the said parties of the second part, their heirs and assigns, at the rate of .....all of the timber now being worked for turpentine purposes upon the following described tract of land situate, lying and being in the County of Leon State of Florida for the purpose of boxing, working and otherwise using said timber for turpentine purposes:

* * * and the West Half of Southeast Quarter, Section 23, Township 2 South, Range 1 East, containing 160 acres more or less.

TO HAVE AND TO HOLD, box, work and otherwise use said timber for turpentine purposes unto the said parties of the second part, their heirs and assigns. And it is hereby expressly covenanted and agreed that the said parties of the second part may commence boxing, working or otherwise using the said timber for turpentine purposes, or any portion thereof Jan. 1st, 1927, and shall have the right to continue to work or otherwise use the said timber, and every portion thereof, for the full term of one year, beginning Jan. 1st, 1927, it being the intention of the parties that this lease shall continue to operate until all of the timber now being worked and each and every part thereof, has been worked and otherwise used for turpentine purposes for the full period of one year from Jan. 1st, 1927. And it is hereby further covenanted and agreed that the said parties of the second part, their heirs and assigns, shall have the free and unrestricted right to enter upon, occupy and use the said land for the purpose of boxing, working and otherwise using the timber thereon for turpentine purposes as aforesaid during the continuance of this lease. And it is further covenanted and agreed that said parties of the second part may have the right at any time to assign this lease in whole or in part, and that any assignee of this lease shall have the same right of assignment, and that all the rights and privileges of said parties of the second prt shall vest in whomsoever may succeed to the interest hereby conveyed to said parties of the second part. And the said party of the first part, for his heirs, executors and administrators, the said granted and leased timber, with the right to box, work and otherwise use the same for turpentine purposes, unto the said parties of the second part, their heirs, and assigns, will forever warrant and defend.

SIGNED & SEALED in the presence of one witnesses.

ACKNOWLEDGED December 20, 19__, in Leon County, Florida, before W. M. Lawhon, J. P. (Seal).

Epitaph on a stone in an old camp cemetery: Beneath this stone old Abraham lies, nobody laughs and nobody cries. Where he is gone and how he fares, nobody knows and nobody cares.

Cottage Beer

Wheat bran - 1 peck
Cane syrup - 2 quarts
Water - 10 gallons
Yeast - 2 Tbs.
Hops - 3 handfuls

Pour boiled bran and hops in the water until both bran and hops sink to the bottom. Then strain through a muslin sheet. When lukewarm, put in syrup and stir until the syrup is melted. Then put in a cask and add the yeast. When fermentation ceases, bung up. In four days it is ready. Drink as the urge hits you.

Face on a tree that is in the second year of being worked. On the right is a face that has been worked out. The tree was not large enough to accept a second face so it was given a break and time to grow. The later methods of turpentining did not affect the quality of lumber which a tree would produce, except that portion within the turpentine face. In the early years of the industry, forests were often seriously damaged by working trees which were too small or by working them too hard. The number of years which a tree could be worked depended largely on its size when it was first chipped. The trees would yield the most in Naval Stores and quite often in timber if the growing trees were worked two or three times, one face each time, with a few years of rest between. When a tree was properly turpentined its normal growth was not retarded more than 20 or 30 percent. (A)

Accumulation of scrape on the face of a tree. At the top are new streaks that the scrape has not formed on. By fall, the trees would have a half inch thick layer of scrape on the face. (A)

A two faced tree that was sawed off above the cups, aprons and gutters to avoid cutting into the nails, which were usually not removed as the cups were moved up. (A)

"Geraldine, I could learn to love you." "Oh go on, Percy, you haven't got money enough to pay for the education."

A woman went to the old turpentine camp school to teach the children in a one room school house, ungraded. She was calling the roll and about halfway down the roll she came to a name that was just simply "F. Jones." After a little boy answered to the name she called him up front and said, "Son, what is your full name?" He grinned at her bashfully, exposing bright ivory teeth. "My name is Fertilizer Jones, ma'am." "What? What did you say?" His face began to pucker up. "Fertilizer. Fertilizer Jones, ma'am." And he showed indications of dissolving into tears. "That can't be your real name." The boy boo-hooed aloud now. The teacher shook an indignant head. "I won't have you called by any such absurd nickname. Stop your crying, go home at once and bring your mother here and I'll soon find out what your real name is." The abject little boy sidled willfully out the door. An hour later, an immense woman appeared abruptly in the doorway. "Good morning ma'am, you was wanting to see me?" Her manner was as friendly as a buzzard. "Why yes, if you're the mother of that little fine looking boy," (A little flattery never hurt anyone's cause.) "What is his name, by the way?" The mollified mother beamed blushingly. " That's little Fertilizer, ma'am." The teacher, with an inward shrinking despair, smiled. "How ever did you choose such an odd name for a child?" The mother was completely won by the teacher now. " You see, ma'am. My old man's name is Ferdinand and my name is Eliza. So we just named the little boy after both of us - Ferdeliza Jones."

Old cat face with resin balls on either side. These balls were chewed like chewing gum for their medicinal value. (A)

The turpentine shanty was a simple building, about ten feet long and six feet wide, which had a roof, sides and back on it, with the front open. It was built of the most simple material, old saw mill slabs for the sides and back with tin for the roof. It provided a place for the hands to get out of inclement weather and a shady place to eat lunch. Some shanties had benches so the hands could sit and rest after lunch. (A)

The sap wood around an old face before it rotted off. The face, because of scarring, would become fat lighter "lightered" and would not rot. (A)

A stranger come into town and asked an old hand that was sitting on the commissary porch if he knowed where the Church of God was at. "Let me see," the old hand said, scratching his head, "down two blocks on the right is Mr. Jones' church. Over on Main Street is Mr. Smith's church. And then there's Mr. Hall's church over on D Street. You know, I just don't believe God got a church here in this town."

An old turpentine hand went to the doctor. The doctor gave him definite instructions on what he should do. Shaking his head, he was about to leave when the doctor said, "Hey, George, you forgot to pay me." "Pay you for what, Boss?" "For my advice," replied the doctor. "No sir, I ain't goin' to take it." So he just shuffled on out the door.

Ox and wagon. During the early years of turpentine the barrels of gum were brought out of the woods by mule or ox and wagon, which was the primary mode of transporting it to the stills until about 1925. At that time the operators began using a one ton sized truck. During the Depression they used a "Hoover wagon" which was mule or ox drawn and built basically the same as the wood spoke wheeled wagon except it had rubber tires on it, which were salvaged from old junk trucks or cars. Named for President Hoover, it came into use during the Depression, for economic reasons. (FDS)

Corn Meal Mush

Corn meal mush is good made this way: Put fresh water in a kettle over the fire to boil and put in some salt and a dash of sugar. When the water boils, stir in handful by handful of cornmeal until it is thick enough to use. In order to have a good mush, the meal should be allowed to cook well and as long as possible while it is thin and before the final handful is added.

Breakfast Cake

1 cup milk
1 pint flour
3 eggs
1 tsp soda
2 tsp cream of tartar
1 piece of butter, about the size of an egg

You can bake it in the oven or in front of the open fire.

Beef Tea

Cut lean tender beef into small pieces. Put them in a bottle. Cork and set in a pot of cold water and then put it on the stove and boil for one hour. Season it to your taste.

Cornbread

1/2 pint buttermilk
1/2 pint sweet milk
If you use sour milk, sweeten it with 1/2 teaspoon soda. Beat two eggs, white and yolk, together. Pour the milk into the eggs, then thicken with about 9 tablespoons of sifted cornmeal. Put a skillet on the stove with a piece of lard about the size of an egg. When melted, pour the batter in the lard in the pan. Add about a tablespoon of salt. Stir it around so it will grease the pan and mix the lard into the batter. Bake in a moderate oven until light brown.

Turpentine tree prepared for the winter, with the straw raked away from it and the cup turned upside down. The hoe was used for pulling the straw and grass away from the tree, which was called "raking the boxes." It was a practice on most tracts being turpentined to remove the straw, grass, chips and brush from around each tree that was cupped. This would lessen the damage in case of fire since fewer of the faces were burned. (A)

Often the forests were control burned after trees had been raked. When this was done the fire was set when the litter on the forest floor was damp and at a time when there was little or no wind blowing. It costs much more to rake the trees than to provide good fire protection. Since fires were so prevalent in the turpentine region it was very important at the end of each season to use some method of control.

Controlled burning in the turpentine woods at night. It is a beautiful sight to watch the fire creeping through the big pines on a clear, cool night. Wild fire was a constant menace to turpentine timber. The damage done by wild fire cost the timber land owners of the South an estimated $25 million annually. Trees with highly flammable faces which were covered with crude gum were very susceptible to damage by fire. An uncontrolled fire in a forest that was being worked for turpentine could do untold damage. Not only were small seedlings killed, but large trees were often damaged to the extent that they would die. Uncontrolled fire also melted the zinc on the galvanized cups, gutters and aprons, thus exposing the tin, which would rust. Raw gum contaminated with rust from rusty cups, gutters and aprons was likely to lower the quality of rosin as much as three or four grades. Trees with faces that had burned destroyed the coating of gum and were often attacked by turpentine borers. When a large number of these insects bored into the heart of a tree they damaged it enough that it was often blown down by the first strong wind. In some areas, 100% of the burned faces showed that borers had entered the trees. Faces that were burned healed very slowly. (A)

Calf's Liver and Bacon

Cut the liver into slices and fry it first. Then fry the bacon. Lay the liver in a dish and the bacon on top of it. Serve it up with gravy made in the pan with boiling water, thickened with flour, butter and lemon juice. A little parsley and onion may be chopped into it or a little boiled parsley stewed over the liver. Garnish with slices of lemon.

Cooked Ham

Scrape the ham clean. Do not put into cold nor boiling water. Let the water become warm, then put the ham in. Simmer or boil lightly for five or six hours. Take out and shave the rind off. Rub granulated sugar into the whole surface of the ham, so long as it can be made to receive it. Place the ham in a baking dish with a bottle of cider. Baste occasionally with the juice and let it bake an hour in a gentle heat. A slice from a nicely cured ham done this way is enough to animate the ribs of death. Or, having taken off the rind, stewed bread crumbs or raspings over it so as to cover it, set it before the fire or in the oven until the bread is crisp and brown. Garnish with carrots, parsley and so forth. The water should simmer all the time and never boil fast.

Preparing Pig's Cheek for Boiling

Cut off the snout, clean the head, divide it. Take out the eyes and the brain. Sprinkle the head with salt and let it drain for 24 hours. Salt it with common salt and saltpeter. Let it lie nine days if to be dressed without stewing with peas, but less if to be dressed with peas - and it must be washed first and then simmer until all is tender.

Morning view of the area that was burned the night before. Within a week after the burn, the wire grass will come back and be green and fresh. The ashes and fresh grass are enjoyed by the wild animals and range cows that graze the area. Notice the small longleaf pine. Unless the fire is extremely hot it is not injured when burned. All of the straw can be burned off a longleaf and it will continue to grow. Control burning was necessary during turpentining in order to keep the woods clear enough of underbrush, snakes, spiders and other varmints so that the hands could work. Control burning would also prevent an uncontrolled wild fire from damaging the trees. (A)

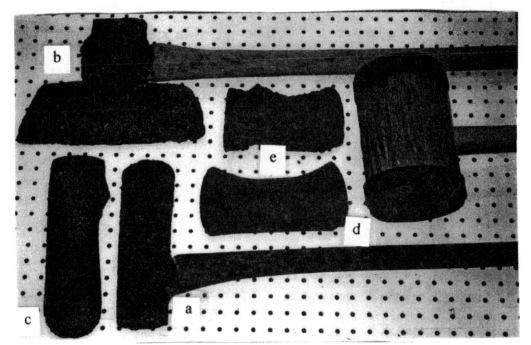

Axes excavated from around turpentine camps. a. Box ax used for cutting an 8"-10" hole into the base of the tree before the cup was invented. The box would hold two quarts of gum. Using this ax, one hand could box about 60 trees in a day. b. Broad axes, which were used to make a cut in the tree for placing the gutter and apron. This operation was usually done by two hands, one held the ax in place and the other pounded it with a wood maul. c. Box ax without handle. d. Double blade felling ax. e. Single blade felling ax. (A)

Corned Beef

Make the following pickle: Two gallons of water, 2 1/2 pounds of salt, a quarter of a pound of syrup, a pound of sugar, 1 1/2 ounces of saltpeter and one quarter ounce of pearlash. Boil all of it together. Skim and pour the pickle on about 25 pounds of beef. Let it stay in it a few days. Boil in plenty of water when cooked to remove the salt. Eat with plenty of vegetables. It is nice to eat cold and also makes a good sandwich.

Round of Beef

This should be carefully salted and wet with pickle juice for 8 to 10 days. The bone should be cut out first and the beef skewered and tied up to make it quite round. It may be stuffed with parsley, in which case the holes to admit the parsley must be made with a sharp, pointed knife and the parsley coarsely cut and stuffed in tight. As soon as it boils it should be skimmed and, afterwards kept boiling very gently.

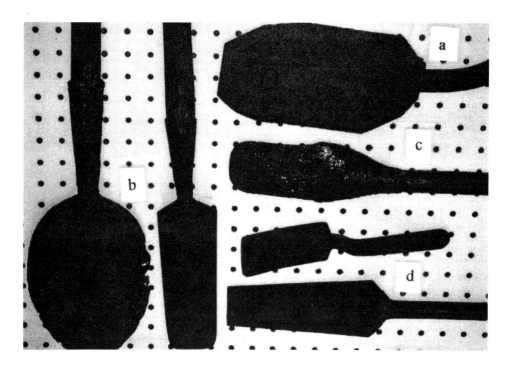

Dip Irons. a and b. Hand forged dip irons used to dip gum out of the boxed trees before the invention of the cup. **c.** Hand forged dip iron used for dipping gum out of cups. **d.** factory made dip irons of two different types that were used for dipping gum out of the metal cups. (A)

NOTE: All of the a and b type dip irons excavated by the author through the years have been hand forged and most are badly deteriorated.

Johnny Cakes

1 pint cornmeal
1 pint sweet milk
1 teacup flour
1 Tbs. syrup
2 eggs
1 Tbs. melted butter
a little salt
1 tsp soda
1 tsp cream of tartar

Bake it in a moderate oven in a square cast iron tin.

This jack-leg preacher was talking to a fellow about the judgment day coming. "When is it?" "I don't know," the preacher said, "it could be tomorrow or it could be the next day." "Well, don't tell my wife," the fellow said, "she'll want to go both days."

The camp boss was questioning a prospective hand on different things to see how he'd react, how far it was from the earth to the moon. The hand looked at him funny and says, "Boss, if you're gonna put me on that drift, I don't want this job."

48

Push down scrape irons used to remove the accumulated gum from a low face. (A)

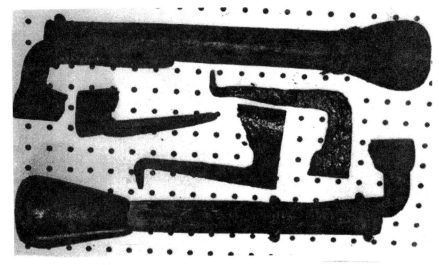

Hack and hogals. Notice the short handle with the steel weight on the end of it. The hack was mounted on a short handle so it could be used to cut the streak into the lower part of the face. Normally, when the hand was using it, he was in a squatting position. The hogal, built almost like the hack (with a wider blade) was used to remove the bark from the tree just above the ground before placing the first cup. (A)

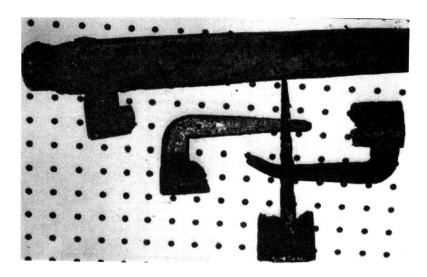

Pull used to make the streak on the tree after the face got above about five feet. The handle was lengthened as the face height increased. (A)

Spanish Moss Jelly

Spanish moss, 1 ounce with one quart water. Put it together and simmer it down to where it is about a half pint. Add some sugar and a little lemon juice. It may be improved with 1/4 ounce of isinglass. The moss should first be steeped in cold water an hour or two. (Isinglass is prepared from the air bladder of a fish.) You know that times are bad when there is nothing left to eat but Spanish moss seasoned with fish bladder.

Crabapple Jelly

Mash your crabapples and take off the stems. Put in a pot covered with water. Let them boil to a pulp, then turn them in a flannel bag and leave all night to strain, then add one pound of sugar to a pint of juice. Boil ten to fifteen minutes, skim and put in jelly glasses. Crabapples gel easily and make a good tart jelly.

"Papa, what's a monologue?" "A monologue is a conversation between a husband and a wife." "I thought that was a dialog." "Naw, a dialog is where two people are speaking."

Old hand: "What did your wife say when you got in so late last night?"
Young hand: "She never said a word. I was going to have them front teeth pulled out anyhow."

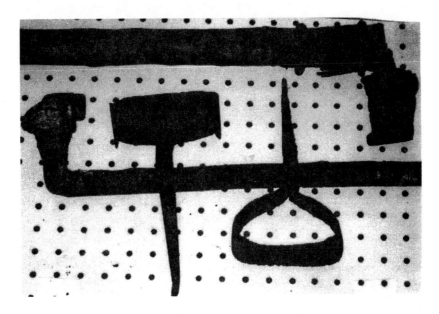

Pull down scrape irons. The scrape iron was used in the fall of the year to remove the accumulated gum from a medium height face. Some operators used these to clean the bark off the tree when beginning a new face. (A)

Syrup Candy

Take one cup of syrup and one cup of water. Combine the ingredients and boil it. Don't stir it until it reaches a hard boil stage. Remove from the fire and let it stand until cool enough to hold in greased hands. Using a small amount at a time, pull the candy back and forth between your hands. After pulling for some time it will change from a brown to a yellowish color, at which time it is done.

Corn Meal Gravy

Take a half cup of lard, toasted corn meal, three glasses of water. Put your lard in the pan on the stove and get it real hot. Add the toasted corn meal, stir it until the meal is brown. Pour the water in and stir it constantly until it is as thick as you would like. If it gets too thick, add more water. If it is too thin, cook it a little longer. This should serve about four people. It goes good on grits or biscuits.

Acid bottle used to spray sulfuric acid on the face with cup cover to protect the galvanized cup from the acid.. The sulfuric acid made the gum flow better from slash pines. Longleaf pine gum ran free without the aid of sulfuric acid. (USDA)

The census taker working a turpentine camp came to one of the houses that was literally crowded with children. Observing a woman bending over a washtub, he addressed her as follows, "Madame, I am the census taker, how many children have you?" "Well, let me see," replied the woman as she straightened up and wiped her hands on her apron, "there's Mary, and Ellen and Della and Susie, and Emma, and Tommy and Albert, and Eddie, and Charlie, and Frank..." "Ma'am," interrupted the census man, "if you could just give me the number." "The number, she exclaimed indignantly, "I want you to understand that we ain't gotten up to numbering them yet, we ain't run out of names."

The young couple got married and were on their way to their honeymoon in the horse and buggy. A black cat ran across the road in front of them and the horse became startled. The new groom said "That's one." A little further down the road they came to a black stump beside the road. Again the horse shied away. The groom said, "That's two." Further down the road a black dog ran across in front of the buggy, again the startled horse jumped around. The new groom got out of the buggy, went up beside the horse, pulled out his pistol and shot the horse. The new bride began to immediately give the groom hell about shooting the horse. The groom looked at her and said, "That's one."

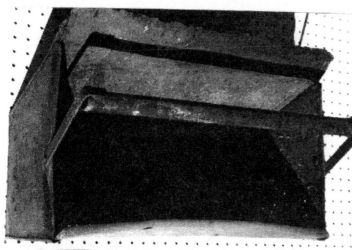

Winged scrape box used to collect scrape at the lower part of the face. The straight part across the back (wing) was placed against the tree. Scrape that was removed with a push down scrape iron fell directly into the scrape bucket. This same bucket was also mounted on two wooden legs about 3' long and used with the pull down scrape iron on medium height faces. (A)

After the producers began using sulfuric acid to enhance the flow of gum from the slash pine a pull with a container to hold the acid was placed on the market. (USDA)

For chest congestion. Melt a little hog lard, put in a small quantity of turpentine. While it is still warm, rub well over the neck, lungs, back and around the nose and ears. Cover the chest and back with flannels.

Cough syrup. Boil pine needles in a little water. Strain off the needles and add enough sugar to make a syrup out of it.

For a head cold, burn a little pine tar on top of the stove in the mornings and breathe the smoke.

For coughs, take 1/2 pint of pine tar, 1 pound of granulated sugar. Put this in a quart of water and boil one hour, slowly. Let it cool and strain. Take 1/2 tsp every three or four hours.

Brawn

Clean a pig's head and rub it over with salt and a little saltpeter. Let it lie two or three days, then boil it until the bones leave the meat. Season with salt and pepper and lay the meat hot in a mold and press and weight it down for a few hours. Boil another hour, covering. Be sure to cut the tongue and lay the slices in the middle as it much improves the flavor.

Dip bucket cup and dip iron show how the dip was taken out of the metal cup and put into the dip bucket. When the bucket was filled with gum it would be dumped into barrels placed throughout the woods. In early years a wooden bucket about the size of a nail keg was used. (A)

"Yo-yo" used for collecting the scrape after the face was above about 6' high. The yo-yo was a small bucket mounted on a handle with a blade on the back of it. The blade scraped the accumulation of gum off the face which fell into the bucket and was then transferred to the scrape bucket. (A)

For developing good, strong teeth, have your children chew rosin balls off the pine trees during the time the teeth are developing.

The way to get rid of flies in the house is to burn pine oil with orange or lemon peelings. They'll go out any opening they can find. If they can't get out the fumes will stupefy them so that they may be gathered up.

Poke

I have heard of poke salad all my life, but we never ate it. We ate only the tender part of the poke plant after the frogs started croaking in the early spring. We would get the new growth of the plant, but not the roots, berries or the tough stems. We took the tender stems of the Spring plant and boiled it. After it boiled we would mix a boiled egg with it and it was real good. If you want to add a little taste to it you might flavor it with some onions or possibly the green tops of spring onions. I have also heard of frying it in butter and mixing with hard boiled eggs.

Dip wagon used for hauling the dip or scrape bucket from tree to tree. A full bucket of dip weighed about 50 pounds. One hand could collect about 30 buckets or seven 31 gallon barrels in a day. (A)

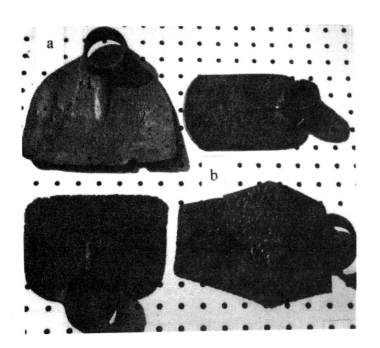

Hoes. a. probably used in the kitchen to make hoe cakes on in front of the fire. This hoe is obviously very old. Look closely and you can see the English Crown. It was excavated from the author's Great-great-great grandmother's home site, which was occupied in the 1820's and 30's. b. Hoes used to "rake the boxes," cut grass and weeds from around the tree and pull it away so that fire couldn't get to the highly flammable turpentine face. (A)

The tree diameter gauge in use indicating that the tree is large enough (9"DBH) to accept a face. (A)

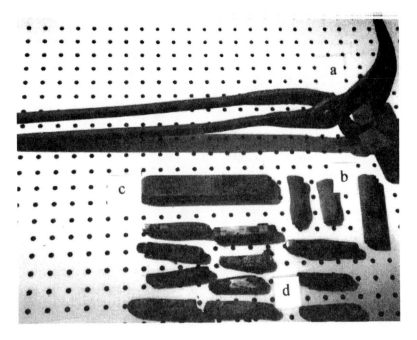

Tin puller for removing the tins and cup nails from the face. It was necessary to remove all metal from the trees, which would damage a saw when the tree was cut for lumber. b. Whetstones used to sharpen the hacks, pulls hogals and scrape irons excavated from turpentine camp sites. c. Whetstone used for sharpening knives and flat blade tools. d. Pocket knives excavated from around the turpentine camp sites. (A)

Baked Pears

Take a dozen tart pears, peel and core them, place sugar and a small lump of butter in the center of each. Put them in a pan with 1/2 pint of water. Bake until tender, basting occasionally with cane syrup while baking. When done, serve with cream.

Rice Fritters

Take 1 pint of rice, cooked, 1/2 cup of sweet milk, two eggs, a tablespoon of flour and a little salt. Have some hog lard hot in a skillet. Allow a tablespoon to each fritter. Fry it brown on each side and turn the same as griddle cakes. If you find the rice splatters in the fat, add a very little more flour. You can judge after frying one.

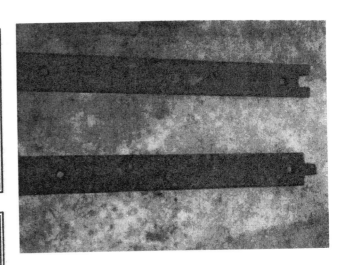

"Snake's head rail" used on railroad tracks from 1825 until about 1850. This rail was used on a logging tram that ran from St. Joe to Lake Wimlico, FL in 1834. The second used was placed into service in 1837 on the Tallahassee-St. Marks railroad. Most trains operated on these early tracks were mule drawn. (A)

Rails and spikes through the years. Right is the 1820's "snakes head" rail with two spikes. Next is a 2 1/2" rail with spikes about 4" long. Next, an 1870's rail typical of the type used on logging trams. Next are the large spike and rail that are still in use. (A)

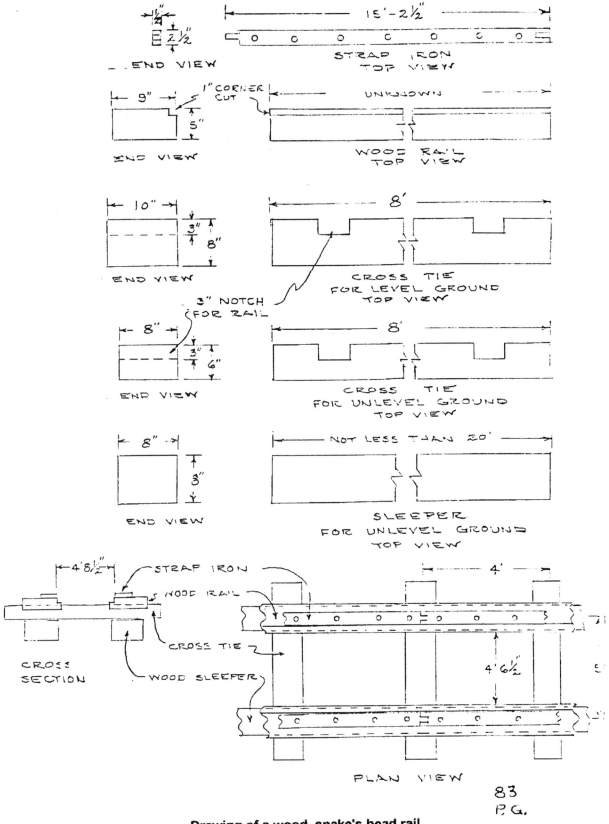

$\frac{1}{4}"$

$2\frac{1}{2}"$

END VIEW

15'-2½"

STRAP IRON
TOP VIEW

9"

1" CORNER
CUT

5"

END VIEW

UNKNOWN

WOOD RAIL
TOP VIEW

10"

3"

8"

END VIEW

3" NOTCH
FOR RAIL

8'

CROSS TIE
FOR LEVEL GROUND
TOP VIEW

8"

3"

6"

END VIEW

8'

CROSS TIE
FOR UNLEVEL GROUND
TOP VIEW

8"

3"

END VIEW

NOT LESS THAN 20'

SLEEPER
FOR UNLEVEL GROUND
TOP VIEW

4'8½"

STRAP IRON

WOOD RAIL

CROSS TIE

WOOD SLEEPER

CROSS
SECTION

4'

4'6½"

PLAN VIEW

83
P.G.

**Drawing of a wood, snake's head rail,
railroad. (A)**

59

Piney woods rooter hog trap used to catch hogs to fatten and kill for food. It was a simple operation to catch a hog. Raise the door in the foreground, tie it up with a rope that went over the board at the top. The rope then went down into the pen and was attached to a stick that was driven into the ground. All of the feed, except a little sprinkling outside and through the gate to lure the hogs in, was placed around the stick. The old piney woods rooter would come in and start rooting around the stick and drop the trap door. Often more than one hog would be caught. The piney woods rooter hog was one of the greatest enemies of the young trees, probably an enemy second only to fire. It ate some of the seeds and destroyed many of the baby longleaf pine trees, rooting them up to feast on the juicy bark of the tap roots. Where these hogs were present, natural reproduction of trees was greatly retarded. (A)

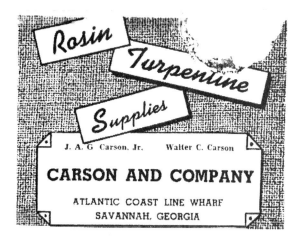

Hog Jowls

The jowls are fatty meat so they are not necessarily used or combined with the souse meat. Some people salt them down and cure them just like hams and save them until warm weather to be boiled in with their vegetables to season them. Others grind them up with their sausage meat. You can fry them, but it is a little tough.

Pig's Feet and Ears

Clean carefully and soak some hours and boil till tender. Then take them out, boil some vinegar and a little salt with some of the water and, when cold, put it over them. When they are to be dressed, dry them, cut the feet in two and slice the ears. Fry and serve with butter, mustard and vinegar. They may be either done in batter or only floured.

The Piney Woods Rooter
Old sow in the corner putting down bread
Pigs outdoors combing their head
Drove the old sow into the house
And there cooked backbones, chit'lins and souse.

There is a story of a turpentine hand who lived in a shack in the pine woods of North Florida. He had some land cleared for farming and considered himself especially lucky because a herd of piney woods rooters ran wild in the woods sustaining themselves on pine masts. One day an agriculturalist visited the old hand and suggested that he get rid of the piney woods rooter and start raising Poland china hogs. The old hand asked " Why should I get shed of them hogs? Ain't costing me nothin to raise them." "Just think of the time" said the agriculturalist, "You can fatten Poland china hogs in six months. It takes two years for those old piney woods rooters to get fat." The old

hand just looked at the agriculturalist sideways and said, "Shucks, time don't mean a dad-blamed thing to a hog."

The piney woods rooter was a principle source of fresh meat for the people of the piney woods. The first cold snap of winter brought hog killing time and, for a while, there was an abundance of fresh pork in the diets of the people, who are said to eat all of the hog but the squeal. Piney woods rooters were prized for making country cured ham, bacon and sausage. The piney woods rooter, after generations of inbreeding and running wild, reverted from what was originally domestic stock. It was designed by nature for ranging in a region where food was scarce. Its proficiency as a forager gave rise to such expressions as the "root hog or die poor days", meaning the reconstruction period. His skull was low and elongated, the snout prolonged and tapering. The neck was scrawny. The back humped at the center and sloped towards the flanks. He had a streamlined appearance that was in keeping with his fleetness, which was almost equal to that of a horse. The piney woods rooter seldom lacked food, even during the worst seasons. Wherever the hogs were numerous quails and snakes were scarce. He would eat bird eggs and snakes of all kinds. It was believed that piney woods rooters were immune to the venom of rattle snakes and moccasins. They also ate mice, rabbits, skunks, possums and many other small animals. In addition to their predatory characteristics, as scavengers the piney woods rooter left no carcass, however putrid. On the vegetarian side, they were fond of corn, peanuts, acorns, roots, palmetto berries and, most of all, pine masts. Some folks used to say that when all other food was gone, the piney woods rooter would eat pine lightwood knots. When in numbers, piney woods rooters were probably in every respect the most dangerous animal to be found in the woods. Many men have had to save themselves by climbing up a tree. Even an armed man, mounted on a horse, was not entirely safe. Turpentine hands had to hang their food in trees to keep the hogs from eating it. Ordinary dogs were no protection and they only invited trouble as they were the hog's pet hatred. When hog killing time came around the serious business of bringing home the bacon began. This was done with the aid of a pack of catch dogs with the men following closely behind on horses. The dogs caught the hogs by seizing them by the ear and holding on until a man arrived with a pigging string to tie them up. The best time for hog killing was said to be on a cold morning when the moon was in its ascendancy. Hogs butchered on such a day were not as likely to dry out or be attacked by blow flies. Piney woods rooters on the open range were a far greater menace to crops than were the cattle and it was much more expensive to build a hog tight fence. In 1937 the Florida Legislature declared wild hogs to be nonexistent in order to put an end to the common excuse used by hog thieves.

Souse Meat

Take one hog's head, salt, 4 teaspoons of black pepper, 2 teaspoons of red pepper, 2 1/2 teaspoons of allspice, 1 teaspoon of cloves and vinegar. Clean the hog's head by removing the snout, eyes, ears and all the skin. Trim off the fat. Cut the head into four pieces and soak it in salt water for three hours to draw out the blood. Drain off the salt water and wash well in cold water. The heart, tongue and other meat trimmings may be cooked with the head meat if you like. Cover meat with hot water and boil until all meat can be removed from the bones. Remove all meat from bones, strain the broth. Add about three tablespoons of salt, the other seasonings, two quarts of broth in which the meat has boiled and mix thoroughly. Cook the mixture 15 or 20 minutes. Pour into a stone crock. Cover with a clean cloth and weight it down. Cool it and then cut into slices as needed. This will make about six pounds of souse.

PAP HENRY was proud of his hog, a sharp-nosed rooter with a razor-edged back. He got the hog on a swapping deal with Sam Henderson. Pap figured he had made a good deal. With a little fattening, the hog would be ready for killing. Pap smacked his lips when he thought of the ham, the souse-meat, and the golden-brown crackling bread he was going to have—come Fall.

But for some unknown reason, the hog refused to fatten. Pap fed him huge amounts—even raiding barns to do it—but the hog remained as sharp-backed and gaunt as ever. In desperation, Sam turned to "Doc," a shriveled old man who was supposed to have great powers. Doc said, "Sho' ah can make yo' hawg fat. Jist feed 'im a pinch uv dis." And he gave Pap a pinch of black stuff that looked and smelled for all the world like snuff.

Pap went home with high hopes. He fed the hog the black, evil-smelling stuff that "Doc" had given him. He didn't notice any difference right away. The hog just kept rooting around, and you could still count his ribs. Disgusted, Pap stomped into the house and went to sleep.

He was awakened by a tremendous snorting out at the barn. Pap leaped to his feet and rushed out the back door. Someone was trying to steal his hog! He tore around the corner of the barn and stopped dead in his tracks. The stuff had worked! *And how* it had worked. The hog was higher than the edge of the barn. His ears were huge, and he kept swinging his snout around and snorting. Pap Henry couldn't believe his eyes. This was more hog than he had ever seen. Then, suddenly, Pap fainted dead away.

It took a lot of talking on the part of the people from the circus to convince Pap that the elephant was not his hog. Patiently, they explained that the elephant had broken away from the circus—and, anyway, he wasn't good to eat. They even pointed out the hog, still sharp-nosed and sharp-backed, asleep in a corner of the barn. When they took the elephant away, Pap was feeding the hog again.

Rattlesnake killed in the author's yard. (A)

Rattlesnake that had caught a full grown rabbit. I guess you could say this indicates that a rabbit should not french kiss a rattlesnake. The author killed this snake one night while walking along an old road. I saw something in the moonlight that appeared to be an alligator with something white in the middle of it so I shined my flashlight on it and saw this rattlesnake coiled around the rabbit. The turpentine hand had to be constantly on the look-out for snakes. Many men have been killed by snakes while working in the woods. It was said that the piney woods rooter hog was immune to the bite of rattlesnakes and moccasins and would often kill and eat them. (A)

Roast Rabbit

Take a young rabbit and dredge it with flour. Cook for half an hour over a brisk fire Take the livers with a bunch of parsley, boil them and chop them up fine together. Melt some butter and put half the liver and parsley into the butter. Pour it in the dish and garnish the dish with the other half. Roast them over the fire until they are light brown.

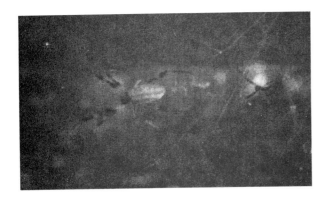

Wood spider. Burning the woods destroys many of these. The old mama spider and it's young spider in the same web. Another hazard that the turpentine hand had to be constantly aware of. (A)

Fox squirrel's nest. They build and live in nests like this throughout natural pine growth timber areas. (A)

Hornet's nest. These are very common in the woods, especially when the woods are not burned. If the woods are burned they will build higher in the trees and won't be a problem to people working in the woods. They were in the same areas as the wasps nests which were often built under the turpentine cups on trees. The yellow jacket, which builds his nest in a hole in the ground, is another hazard to people working in the woods. (A)

Corn Bread Dressing

3/1/2 cups of corn bread crumbs
3 1/2 cups of crumbled biscuits
1/2 cup of butter
1/2 cup of milk
1/2 teaspoon of pepper
2-3 teaspoons of sage
1 egg, slightly beaten
2 or more cups of chicken broth
3 Tablespoons of minced onions
1 cup of chopped celery
2 teaspoons of salt

Mix bread and biscuit crumbs in a large pan or bowl. Melt butter and lightly sauté onions and celery. Add to the crumb mixture. Add the remaining ingredients and mix well. Bake in a well greased shallow pan in a hot oven for 15 to 20 minutes.

RED-COCHADED WOODPECKER NESTING COLONEY AREA PRESERVED ST. JOE PAPER CO.

Red cockaded woodpecker nesting colony sign. This sign is placed on an area preserved for the woodpecker. In the earlier years of the endangered species act, there were five acres reserved for a colony. Now it is up to 20 acres. Consider losing 20 acres of timber land to a bird. That's what happens when one of these colonies is found on your property. The red cockaded woodpecker usually nests in pines that are more than 60 years old. (SJPC)

Turtle (land or water)

Dress your turtle by turning him on his back and cutting the bottom off. A small hatchet should be used to cut the bottom shell down each side between the front and back legs. (Soft shell turtles can be cut with a butcher knife.) Trim all of the meat out from inside the shell. Skin the legs and trim the meat off them. If the turtle has eggs, which it may in the Spring, save them to boil in your soup. The meat is good cooked in a hash the same way as beef, pork or venison. It may also be cooked in a soup with tomatoes. Mama would toast meal in the oven and add it to her soup after it was almost cooked. This would give it consistency and would suffice for a full meal if served with biscuits or corn bread.

Alligator turtle common around the ponds in the piney woods. The turpentine hands had to keep a constant watch for these and many other varmints. He was very slow and would bite if you got too close to him. There's an old saying that when he bit you he would not turn loose until it thundered. The saying was probably made to keep children from playing with turtles. Almost all species of turtles were eaten by the turpentine hands. (A)

Longhorn range cows grazing in the piney woods. It takes about ten acres of this sandy pine land to support one cow. They eat the vegetation that competes with the young pines. Their hooves scar the ground so the pine mast will have a place to germinate. (A)

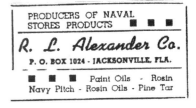

OLIVER LIVE STOCK COMPANY
WHOLESALE AND RETAIL
HORSES, MULES AND CATTLE
—
AUCTION SALES FROM SEPTEMBER TO APRIL
—
LARGEST BARN SOUTH OF ATLANTA
PHONE 622

THOMASVILLE, GA.

December 8, 1930

Dear Sir:

We have assigned to us to sell, Friday December 12th, twenty-five second-hand mules ranging from twelve to fifteen hundred pounds, belonging to the late Thomas Patterson. These mules have been used in the turpentine business. We will also have ten large mules belonging to an Ice Business. Now these mules are consigned to sell at whatever you give. Some of these mules are awful good, and we are sure you will find some real bargains among them. If interested in large mules at all, it will certainly pay you to be here. All are out of work and ready to go to work when you buy.

Remember the date, Friday, December 12th. We start Auction at 10 A. M.

Yours truly,

Oliver Live Stock Company
By W. E. Oliver

For colic in horses or cows, there is no better and quicker relief than a pint of melted hog lard mixed with two tablespoons of turpentine. Make him drink it as warm as possible. If he's not relieved in one or two hours, repeat.

Being told to write an essay on the mule, a small boy turned into his teacher the following effort: "The mule is a hairier bird than the goose or the turkey. It has two legs to walk with, two more to kick with and wears its wings on the side of its head. It is stubbornly backwards about coming forward."

67

BUGGIES
SURRIES
DELIVERY WAGONS
CARTS

FACTORY AND GENERAL OFFICES: EAST POINT, GEORGIA

HIGH GRADE
VEHICLES

ATLANTA, GEORGIA

B.M.BLOUNT, PRESIDENT.
E.R. DUBOSE, VICE-PRES
E.D. DUNCAN, SEC. & TREAS.

August 8, 1930.

Wakulla Turpentine Co.,
Wakulla, Fla.

Gentlemen:

Answering your favor of the 6th, we quoted you on
July 24th as follows:

Axle   Tire
3 1/4 x 3   Steel Skein Turpentine Gears, $90.00 ea.
3 1/4 x 4   "   "   "   "   95.00 ea.

The above prices would be net cash less freight to
Wakulla, or to the 817 Mile Post, St. Marks Branch
S. A. L. Railway, as the freight to both places is
the same, 93¢ per hundred.

As stated in our letter of July 24th, the above
prices, after deducting the freight, would not cover
shop cost, so we offer these gears subject to prior
sale, we hope that you can favor us with your order
promptly, before they are sold.

          Very truly yours,

          WHITE HICKORY WAGON MANUFACTURING CO.

                    President.

BMB/ld

STEEL AXLE TURPENTINE GEAR

Wide track only, 5 feet, center to center of tires on ground.

48 inches between standards.   Linchpin axles.

These gears are made especially for turpentine hauling, having, in addition to
48 inches width between standards and high wheels, the Linchpin axles,
which admit of greater strain in the side motion of the wagon. They
are also especially ironed, adding to the strength of the wagon,
and have heavy bolsters, hounds and tongue. Our turpentine
gears are superior to those made by any other factory and
are not simply farm wagons with wide bolsters and high
wheels, but made especially for the purpose, from a
careful study of the wants of the trade.

Specifications complete include Whiffletrees, stay chains and tongue chains but

no body, seat or brake.

Number	Size of Axle or Skein	Size of Tire	Height of Wheels		Estimated	
			Front	Hind	Weight	Capacity
	STEEL AXLE					
62	1⅝ x 9 in.	3 x ½ in.	3 ft. 8 in.	4 ft. 6 in.	1,000 lbs.	3,000 lbs.
63	1¾ x 10 "	3 x ½ "	3 " 8 "	4 " 6 "	1,100 "	4,000 "
64	1¾ x 10 "	4 x ½ "	3 " 8 "	4 " 6 "	1,100 "	4,000 "
65	2 x 11 "	3 x ½ "	3 " 8 "	4 " 6 "	1,200 "	5,000 "
66	2 x 11 "	4 x ½ "	3 " 8 "	4 " 6 "	1,200 "	5,000 "
	STEELSKEIN					
68	3 x 9 "	3 x ½ "	3 ft. 8 in.	4 ft. 6 in.	1,000 lbs.	3,000 lbs.
69	3¼ x 10 "	3 x ½ "	3 " 8 "	4 " 6 "	1,100 "	4,000 "
70	3¼ x 10 "	4 x ½ "	3 " 8 "	4 " 6 "	1,100 "	4,000 "

Steel Skein Gears have Long Sleeve Steel Skeins with Nuts instead of Linchpins
and Collars.

Mfg. by

White Hickory Wagon M'f'g. Co., East Point, Ga.

"Did you get any replies to the ad you placed for a wife?" "Yeah, I got hundreds of them." "What did they say?" "Oh, nearly all of them came from men who said you can have mine."

A lady to a turpentine hand that wouldn't work: Why don't you work? Hard work never killed anyone.   Turpentine hand: You're wrong ma'am, I lost both my wives that way.

August 11th,1930.

White Hickory Wagon Mfg Company,
East Point,Ga.
Dear Sirs.-

We have yours of the 8th quoteing price on yuor 3½x10 Steel
Skein Turpentine Wagon of $95.00 less freight to our shipping point.

We hand you herewith our check to cover one of these wagons
and would thank you to RUSH shipment to 817 Mile Post,StMarks Branch,
S.A.L.Ry.   Prepay station.

We use your regular order blank.

Very respectfully,

WAKULLA TURPENTINE COMPANY,

By *[signature]*
Sec & Tres.

CARSON NAVAL STORES COMPANY,

LIBERTY NATIONAL BANK & TRUST CO. BUILDING

WAREHOUSE   SAVANNAH,GEORGIA,   BRANCH OFFICE
303 RIVER ST. EAST   JACKSONVILLE, FLA

November 26th. 1930

If you are in need of nails for raising your cups
and aprons send us your orders. We have a complete stock
of the sizes used by Turpentine Operators and will guarantee
that our prices are well in line.

We would also like to call your attention to a new
tool made by the Council Tool Company-- A combination gutter and nail puller, with which one man can pull both gutters and cup nails. These sell for $2.50 each and we recom-
mend them as being practical time and money savers. Let
us send you one for trial - if not entirely satisfactory
you can return for credit with no expense to yourself.

Your orders are appreciated.

Carson Naval Stores Company

70

TART STAVE COMPANY
ROSIN BARREL ST.
AND
CIRCULAR HEAD,
PALATKA, FLORIDA

February 13, 1930.

Mr. M. Culbreth,
Wakulla, Fla.

Dear Mr. Culbreth:

We expect to operate the Rosin Barrel
Stave and Heading Mill in Perry this coming season, and
will be in position to make shipments in carload lots
not later than March 1st.   We expect to furnish nice
long leaf yellow pine Staves, crozed at both ends, with
circular Heading to match.

Our prices will be the same as other
manufacturers prices, and we will be in position to handle
your account in a satisfactory manner and as will best suit
your convenience.   We trust you will favor us with a share
of your business during the coming season, and we will
appreciate anything you may say in your community in our
favor.

Thanking you in advance for any consideration you may give us, with best wishes from the writer,
we are

Yours Very Truly,
TART STAVE COMPANY

By: _F. S. Crathin_

FSC:NJL

71

December 13th, 1932.

Consolidated Naval Stores Company,
Jacksonville, Florida.

Dear Sirs,-

We would be pleased to have you quote us price on clay cups delivered Wakulla, also on Galv gutter strips both at Jacksonville and Wakulla.

We are very much undecided just now whether to put up any new cups this winter or not, but at the present prices of rosin it would seem necessary to either make better grades and more of it or close down altogether. We will have several crops to throw off this winter.

Very respectfully,

WAKULLA TURPENTINE COMPANY.

By

Sec & Tres.

MOBILE STEEL COMPANY

INCORPORATED

IRON AND STEEL

MANUFACTURERS OF

SHEET METAL PRODUCTS

MOBILE, ALA., U. S. A.

GALVANIZED FLAT SHEETS
BLACK FLAT SHEETS
SHEET COPPER, ZINC, BRASS
TIN AND TERNE PLATES
ROOFING SLATE, SLATERS FELT
ROOFING NAILS
TRINIDAD ASPHALT, ROOFING PITCH
GALVANIZED CORRUGATED TANKS
"MSCO" SOLDERLESS EVAPORATORS

TURPENTINE CUPS AND APRONS
GALVANIZED PORTABLE FIREPLACES
METAL ROOFING, SIDING, CEILINGS
GALVANIZED METAL SHINGLES
RIDGE ROLL, GALVANIZED & TIN VALLEY
CONDUCTOR PIPE AND EAVES TROUGH
ELBOWS AND TRIMMINGS
GALVANIZED AWNINGS AND SKYLIGHTS

BARS, PLATES, STRUCTURAL SHAPES, REINFORCING RODS
FABRICATORS
STEEL BUILDINGS, TANKS, BRIDGES

February 5th, 1930

Wakulla Turpentine Co.,
    Wakulla, Fla.,

QUOTATIONS SUBJECT TO CHANGE WITHOUT NOTICE. ALL AGREEMENTS ARE CONTINGENT UPON STRIKES, ACCIDENTS, DELAYS OR CARRIERS AND OTHER DELAYS UNAVOIDABLE OR BEYOND OUR CONTROL

Gentlemen:-

    We thank you very much for your order of February 3rd., which we have entered as follows:-

    Ship to Wakulla Turpentine Company, Wakulla, Fla., Freight prepaid:-

10000 Heavy Galvanized 1½" x 15" Straight Flat Strips
 1000   "   "   2½" x 30"   "   "   "

    Draft through The Exchange Bank, Wakulla, Fla.

    We expect to make shipment of this material immediately and take this opportunity to thank you for this nice order.

    With very best regards, we remain,

        Yours very truly,

        MOBILE STEEL COMPANY, INC.,

        BY: _J. R. Mighell, Jr._
              GENERAL MANAGER

JRM: GC

Wife: Dear, tomorrow is our tenth anniversary. Shall I kill a turkey?
Husband: Naw, let him live. He didn't have anything to do with it.

"Hey, I thought you told me when I hired you that you'd never get tired." " That's right Boss, I always stops and rest before I gets tired."

HIGH BLUFF TURPENTINE CO.

MANUFACTURERS OF NAVAL STORES

C. C. LAND, MANAGER

Sumatra, Florida

Sumatra, Florida
March 8th,
1934

Mr. J. P. Moody,
Wewahotee, Fla.

Dear Mr. Moody:

You will recall that in January of this year I had to answer to a charge of peonage in the Federal Court in Tallahassee which I was successful in securing a release from.

Among the witnesses used by the government was Lee Middleton, who was then working for you, and I have recently been advised that he had never returned home from attending Court, and I would like to find out where he is so that I might advise the Government Agents who inquired of me as to his whereabouts.

If you know or possibly can find out where he is I will certainly deem it a personal favor, and an act of friendship if you will advise, since his seeming disappearance throws somewhat of a suspicion towards me, when I honestly know nothing about him, and have not seen him since I last saw him in the Court Room at Tallahassee.

Too, I have learned that his old lady was now at Shinetown, near Millville, and she claims to know nothing of him. Or, do you know the present whereabouts of old Lee's son Willie Middleton, if I can locate him, I believe he will know where his father is.

Again assuring you that if you can furnish me with information that will throw light on the subject, I will greatly appreciate it and will return the favor when the opportunity presents itself. With kind personal regards, I am,

Yours very sincerely,

C. C. LAND, SUMATRA, FLA.

For appendicitis, take one ounce of olive oil, three times a day. Rub turpentine on your side to take out the pain.	For boils, take a piece of rosin and 1/3 as much lard. Melt the two together. Put this plaster on boils and it will draw out the core.

WAKULLA TURPENTINE COMPANY

MANUFACTURERS OF

PURE GUM TURPENTINE AND ROSIN

WAKULLA, FLORIDA

April 10th,1920.

Carson Naval Stores Company,
Savannah,Ga.
Gentlemen.-

 We are in receipt of your letter of the 4th inst in answer to our inquiry of the 2nd for prices on spirit barrels,and note that you could furnish us a car at $3115 delivered.

 The same day wecwrote you a representative of Palatka Cooperage Company called at our place with a price of $3.15 with Live Oak freight, but finally agreed to ship and guarantee the price against any legitmate competition,so as we were needing the barrels right away we give him an order with the understending that we may deduct,when remitting,thy difference in the price charged and the price we could buy them at lator.

 However, we are giving you credit for making the price and to show our appreciations we consigned to you at Jacksonville 35 B/R and 10 Casks spirits to be handled for our acct.

     Yours truly,

    WAKULLA TURPENTINE COMPANY,

    By

      Sec & Tres.

A book agent came by the old farmer's house, selling Scientific Agriculture books. The old man thumbed through them. He said, "No, I don't want them." "You ought to buy these books, sir. If you had these books you could farm twice as good as you do today." The old fellow settled himself more comfortably in his chair, "Hell, son, I don't farm half as good as I know how to now."

Three boys were bragging about how rich their fathers were. The first boy said " My daddy owns a hundred acres of turpentine trees." The next boy said, "That's nothing, my daddy owns two hundred acres of turpentine trees." The third boy said, "My daddy owns more than both of yours, when he came in at 3:00 am, mamma gave him hell."

CAMP

The main turpentine camp was usually located many miles from the nearest town on a 40 acre or larger tract of land. It contained a fire still, commissary, workers' quarters, slightly better housing for supervisory personnel, occasionally a juke, school and church. A series of smaller outlying "side camps" containing worker's quarters were placed throughout the crops on larger operations.

Camp beds were made of ticking, which was a strong light blue cloth with white stripes through it. The ticking was sewn together on the ends and one side, then stuffed with dried Spanish moss, after which the remaining side would be sewn. Sleeping on the bed was about like sleeping on a pile of rocks. Sometimes the wood framed bed had wire with springs on the sides to allow the mattress to give a little. They were taken out and sunned occasionally, the moss loosened up and the bed bugs removed from them. Pillows were made of the same ticking material with duck, goose or chicken feathers for a filler. (The same material was also used for making pigging strings to tie piney woods rooter hogs with when caught in the woods. We would tear the ticking into strips 1" wide, tie three of the hog's legs with it and leave him beside the road to be picked up later.)

The "pairing off" of couples was usually done by The Man, who was the woods rider, and ran the camp and the commissary. He also officiated at "commissary weddings" or weddings held in the camps on Saturday afternoons. The local justice of the peace would sometimes come and officiate at the weddings. Occasionally a couple of the hands would get together, go into the nearest town and get what they called a "pair of license" and have a "cote-house weddin". However, most of the weddings were performed at the camp.

On Saturday nights the hands would dance, play their drums and other crude musical instruments and have a good time. They would end the night drinking some 'shine and sitting under the trees gambling with their commissary money. If it happened to be a family man who had more need of his money, he may lose all the money that he'd just gotten paid. There was always some slick character that went from camp to camp and did nothing but gambled. After a profitable night, he would turn his winnings in at the commissary and buy himself things that he could take to other places and trade for real currency.

There was no law in the camps. If the hands got into a fight and cut each other up or shot each other, there was nothing done about it as far as the law was concerned. The only time the law would come was when one man killed another, then they would come from the county seat to the camp and investigate. Usually it ended up that it was a matter of killing in self-defense and no charges were filed. These same people that gambled and fought on Saturday night would go to church together on Sunday and have a big time. Sunday evenings we could hear the beating of drums at the church, which was three miles from our home. When we got within a mile of the church we could hear the singing.

Once my truck got stuck in the sand near the Delph Quarters camp on a Sunday afternoon. I could hear the drum at the church so I walked there to get help. The people invited me into the church and told me if I'd just have a seat and wait they'd help me. They gave me a seat on the front row and went back to beating their drums, singing, and enjoying life. It seemed strange to see the people that had been fighting on Saturday night together at church, singing and having a big time on Sunday afternoon. The services usually went on all day and into the night. Two of the male hands "got the spirit" while I was there that evening. They were talking but I couldn't understand what they were saying. The old church building had cypress poles supporting the center of the roof. The two big men climbed those poles all the way to the top of the building. They had big balls of sweat popping off their bodies and were soaking wet when they came down. In the meantime, all the other people were singing, dancing, beating the drums and having a good time. The old jack-leg, fire and damnation preacher was doing his amen thing. He wasn't preaching from a pulpit, he was walking up and down the aisle stomping his feet so hard it made the building shake. All of the children were gathered in a corner, obviously afraid of him. That trip to church was an education in itself to me to see how these people worshipped and did their religious things. Actually, the preacher was preaching from the Bible and some of the songs they were singing were hymns that I recognized. About 9:00 p.m. the services were over and some of the men went with me and pushed my old truck out of the sand.

I had an occasion to go to church with these people one other time, which was to the funeral of one of the old hands who I knew only as "Big Boy." Before he died I went to see him and was surprised that his wife let me in because I was no more than a boy. His skin was breaking open on his body and he looked in real pitiful shape. I'll never forget the sight of him. A few days later I went to his funeral. They had put him in a pine box which was lined with real pretty cloth, and placed him down at the front of the church. All of the people passed by and looked at him, even with him looking as bad as he did. The service lasted for two or three hours with the people all doing the same singing, beating drums, and having a good time - the way they had done at Sunday services.

Pay day was Saturday afternoon. The hands would gather at the commissary where The Man would take the tally man's records and pay each man in accordance to what the records indicated he had done during the week. In the late 1930s a good male turpentine hand was paid about $10 to $12 a month, with a female usually being paid about $2 a month. The woods rider received around $30 a month. They were also furnished their housing and were allowed to buy on credit at the commissary. They could only spend their money in the commissary, buying goods that the company had brought to sell to them. It is said that some company owners would make money by buying groceries at wholesale and selling to the hands at retail price, while using their own script or "commissary money" to deal with. The commodities supplied at the commissary suggests that most meals of the turpentine hands probably consisted of corn bread, cured pork, black coffee, grits, beans, syrup and biscuits. Local game and fish were taken in so-called leisure time, when the time was available. Berries, grapes, persimmons, nuts and other edible wild plants were gathered in season. Notice the Wholesale Grocery Co. receipt dated 4/19/39. The first item is 1/2 Bbl of Ruby Rose wine at $2.78. The wine was almost always the first item on the many weekly receipts that I have reviewed.

The typical camp had a common drinking water well that was shared by all with a washing shed nearby for washing clothes.

A typical day's work for the turpentine hand was from "can to cain't". He would rise about 5:30 a.m., eat a meal that was usually prepared the night before, then head to the woods at first light. Around 11:30, he ate a light lunch that was packed the night before, which he carried to the woods with him, usually in a metal syrup bucket. He worked until nearly sundown, then walked back to the camp for supper and to do his home chores. This ritual was performed five or six days a week, depending on how fast each of his prescribed jobs got done.

The yards around the buildings were swept clean of any straw, leaves or grass by the women and children, using gallberry bush brooms (gallberry bushes tied together). Sweeping the yards clean was necessary to keep woods or building fires from spreading. Every house had chickens in the yard that scratched in the sand to get most of their food, but were also fed scraps left from meals. Every hand had his hogs, which were usually kept in a pen away from the buildings. They, too, were fed scraps. I'm reminded of the hand that got an old sow and half a dozen pigs. He didn't have water for them so each morning, before he went to the woods to work, he would take three of the pigs and the old sow and load them in a wheelbarrow, carry them down to the pond, let them drink and wallow around in the pond for a while. Then he'd load them into the wheelbarrow and carry them back to the pen. Then he'd take the other three pigs, carry them to the pond, let them wallow around and get a drink, then carry them back to the pen. The tally man saw him doing this and asked him, " Why don't you let those hogs out and drive all of them down to the pond at the same time rather than hauling them back and forth twice a day like this in the wheelbarrow. It takes a lot more time to haul them back and forth, than it would to turn them out and drive them all at once. Just look at all the time you're wasting." The old hand just looked at the tally man and said, "Shucks, boss, you know time jus' don't mean a thing to a hog."

I've gone back to hunt artifacts at many of the camps that I visited as a boy while riding the woods hunting cows. These camps were located in the same areas that the Indian villages had been before them. The Indians and camp owners had the same common needs, high ground and a fresh water supply. There was a side camp called Seven Shanties near a spring and sinkhole that was named for the seven buildings needed to house the hands to work the area. Deeper into the woods was a camp called Tin Top, where the buildings actually had tin roofs. The Pin Hook camp, near our home, had a commissary, church, school, several houses and a big turpentine still. There was a large camp and still near the Aucilla River, called Flint Rock, built in an area where the Indians had lived many years earlier. The ground was covered with flint chips left by the Indians chipping their tools and points. Flint Rock was probably the largest camp in this area. At one time it had a post office as well as all other buildings necessary to make it self-sustaining. All of these camps were accessible to the tram roads that belonged to the Live Oak, Perry and Gulf Railways. The line ran from Live Oak west to the coast then south to a camp called Mandalay on the Aucilla River. From there, it continued South to Hampton Springs, which in the early years was a resort town with a hotel, and then on into Perry. The logging and turpentine operators used these tram roads, which were built in the 1870's and 80's, for many years, even during the years of working the second growth timber.

I married a widow with a grown daughter. My father fell in love with my stepdaughter and married her, thus becoming my son-in-law and my stepdaughter became my mother because she was my father's wife. My wife gave birth to a son, which was, of course, my father's brother-in-law and my uncle, well he was the brother of my stepmother. My father's wife became the mother of a son, he was, of course, my brother and also my grandchild, for he was the son of my daughter. Accordingly, my wife was my grandmother, because she was my mother's mother. I was my wife's husband and grandchild at the same time and as the husband of a person's grandmother is his grandfather. I am my own grandfather.

The editor of the weekly journal lost two of his best subscribers. They wrote to him and asked for a remedy for their respective troubles. Number 1, the happy father of twins wrote to inquire the best way to get them carefully over teething. Number 2 wanted to know how to protect his garden from grasshoppers. The editor framed his answers upon the lines, but unfortunately transposed the two names, with the result that Number 1, who was blessed with twins read in reply to his inquiry, "cover them carefully with straw and set fire to them and the little pests, after jumping about in the flames for awhile, will speedily be settled." Number 2, plagued with grasshoppers, was told to give them a little castor oil and rub their gums gently with a bone ring.

Two-holer outhouse, typical of the turpentine and logging camp types. Shared usually by two families. In excavating around old camp sites, I have had no problem finding where they were located. They were almost always south of the houses because the prevailing wind direction is from the northwest. There were holes dug under the outhouse to accept the droppings and often the houses were moved from one place to another and placed over a different hole. When they were moved, the abandoned hole was filled with trash from around the camp and covered over with sand. Many of my artifacts came from these abandoned holes. I found a complete sewing machine, patent date 1856, that was taken apart, placed in the hole and covered over. No, it is not a good place to dig if you are bothered by the thought. All of the droppings have long since gone back to the earth, leaving only the glass and better metals. (A)

Green Vegetables

All of the green vegetables, turnips, mustard, collards, green beans, etc. were cooked basically the same way. Simply cooked in a pot of boiling water over an open fire or on top of the stove. They were almost always seasoned with a slab of salt pork and black pepper.

Potato Cakes

Take 1/4 pound of grated ham, 1 pound of mashed potatoes and a little tallow (suet, beef fat). Mix with the yolk of two eggs, pepper, salt and nutmeg. Roll it into little balls or cakes and fry it to a light brown in lard. Sweet herbs may be used in place of ham. Plain potato cakes are made with potatoes and eggs only.

Collard patch. All of the hands had their collard patch for greens. It was usually located near the kitchen door so the cook could get leaves to season other foods with and dish water could be used to water the plants. (A)

Coal oil lamp used over the author's writing table at "the river house". This type of lamp used kerosene, coal oil, pine oil or whale oil for lighting the camp house. (A)

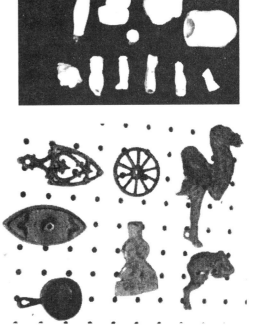

Doll parts, heads, legs, arms, and the belly portion of a doll. Also parts of children's toys, hatchet, the back of a horse, the front of a camel, trivet, iron, pan and wheel. (A)

Cast iron stove with pots and pans similar to those used in the quarters houses. On the floor left of the stove is a bean pot. In front of the stove is a muffin or bread pan. The meals were cooked inside on the stove during winter and outside over an open fire in summer. I have uncovered many outside cook pits while excavating around camp sites. The pit was easily recognized by its cone shape, burned wood, animal teeth, etc. (A)

Potato Bread

4 potatoes, mashed up real fine
4 tsp of salt
2 quarts lukewarm milk
1/2 cake yeast, dissolved in 1/2 cup warm water
add flour, enough to make a pliable dough

Mold dough with your hands, greased with lard. Place in pan. When it is sufficiently light, it is ready for baking. Bake in a moderate oven until brown.

Pear Fritters

1 pint milk
as much flour as will make a batter
3 eggs
salt to please

Beat yolk and whites of eggs separately. Add yolks to milk. Stir in the whites when mixing the batter. Half tender pears, and core and cut into large thin slices. Lay sliced pear in the center of each quantity of batter. Ladle into a spider of hot hog lard and fry until light brown.

Part of a large collection of bottles dating back to the mid 1800's excavated from camp sites. These are usually found in holes and are seldom unbroken. Many more bottles could be thrown in the outhouse hole if they were broken. (A)

Coffin tacks excavated from a camp site. Big headed tacks used for fastening the cloth liner inside a casket. (A)

Pieces of clay pipes that were excavated at turpentine camps. The one on the lower left has a man's leg on it, with a woman on the other side of the bowl. (A)

Typical quarters house. The front porch and the back "shed room" were added later. The main body of the house was only about 14 feet wide and 18 feet across, with shutters on the windows. The chimney was for a cook stove inside. The original roof was of cypress shingles, overlaid later with galvanized tin. The earlier houses for the hands were often one room pole structures with no floor or windows. If a hand's family was large, a lean-to was added along one wall for additional sleeping space. Each shanty occupant or family had a small garden of vegetables to supplement their diet. Some had a few hogs to butcher for meat and a cow for milking. The camp buildings were almost always considered temporary because as soon as the trees in the area were worked out, the people would be moved to another location. (A)

Flour Gems

1 quart sweet milk
1 tsp cream of tartar
1 cup syrup
a little salt
1 tsp soda

Mix the cream of tartar and the flour. Mix the soda and the milk and make it all stiff with the flour as will make it drop easily from the spoon. Drop it into hot lard and fry.

Corn Oysters

Take 1/2 dozen ears of sweet corn, those which are not too old. With a sharp knife, split each row of the corn in the center of the kernel, lengthwise. Scrape out all the pulp. Add 1 egg, well beaten, a little salt, 1 tablespoon of sweet milk, flour enough to make a pretty stiff batter. Drop in hot hog lard and fry to a delicate brown. If the corn is quite young, omit the milk, using as little flour as possible.

$1.00, 50, 25, 10 and 5 cent piece commissary coins from the Pin Hook Co., Newport, FL,. The Pin Hook Company was a logging and turpentine company that worked the virgin timber in the area between the St. Marks and Wacissa Rivers in Wakulla and Jefferson Counties, FL. They closed their operation in this area and moved to Nassau County, FL in 1900. The hands were paid with company money which could only be used at the company store "commissary." (A)

Back during the second world war I went to town with my Aunt, who was a pretty, young thing back in those days. She was driving an old '38 Chevrolet that belonged to my Granddaddy. We had made our trip to town and were on the way back home when we had a flat tire. All the tires were bald anyway because we were not able to get tires during the war. A couple of soldiers from the nearby base came by and stopped to change the tire for us. When we got home my Aunt was telling my mother about the soldiers stopping and helping to change the tire and my mother said "Well, did they ask you for a date?" My Aunt said "No, they didn't ask me for a date. I'm so country they could probably smell turpentine on my breath."

Pork Loin

Score it and joint it so that the chops may separate easily. Cover it with water. Simmer until almost done, then peel off the skin and coat it with the yolk of an egg and bread crumbs. Roast for fifteen or twenty minutes until it is done.

Roast Leg of Pork

Choose a small leg of young pork. Cut a slit in the knuckle with a sharp knife and fill the space with sage and chopped onion, and a little salt and pepper. When half done, score the skin in slices, but don't cut deeper than the outer rind. Serve it with applesauce and potatoes.

Fried Cakes

3 eggs
salt
1 cup sugar
nutmeg
1 pint new milk
flour, enough to permit the spoon to stand upright in the mixture

Add 2 teaspoons of baking powder and beat until very light. Drop by the tablespoonful into boiling lard and fry.

Cookies
2 cups brown sugar
2 eggs
1 cup butter
1 tsp soda
1/2 cup sweet milk
flour, enough to roll it all out.
Bake on a tin in a moderate oven.

Other items excavated from around camp sites. Mortar and pestle, cast iron kettle, stove eye, and a small cook pot. (A)

The insurance man came by the old turpentine hand's house to collect on his insurance. The old turpentine hand had this rooster that had lost all of his feathers off the lower part of his body. The turpentine hand had his wife make a flannel suit to put on the rooster to keep him from getting too cold during the nights. The rooster was walking around the yard with his flannel suit on. The insurance man says, " Man, that's some thing on that rooster. That's amazing. What did you do?" The old hand told him, " The rooster lost all his feathers off his tail parts so I had my wife build a flannel suit so he wouldn't get cold" " That is amazing, I have never seen anything like that." "Oh man, that's not anything. You ought to see him trying to unzip that thing when he catches an old hen ."

Beads, home made marbles, buttons (some made of oyster shell and bone), and a cold cream jar with a glass lid. (A)

Items that were excavated from around the turpentine camps. Top is a perfume atomizer dated 1902. On the right is the seal of a druggist of Newport, FL who died in 1869. When I opened the seal and found who it belonged to I knew where his gravestone marker was located. Other items are suspender clips, buttons, marbles, beads and belt buckles. The glass item in the center is a bottle "stopper" (cap). The comb is made of bone. (A)

The first known school to be located in what is now Wakulla County, FL was advertised on December 19, 1828 in the Magnolia Advertiser, a weekly newspaper printed in the town of Magnolia. Magnolia was on the St. Marks River, 7 miles upriver from what is now St. Marks. The ad read as follows: "*Tuition. A subscriber has opened a school in Magnolia for the instruction of youth in the various branches of an English education and solicits the patronage of those disposed to encouraged the cultivation of learning in this vicinity. Terms made known at the subscriber's room. Signed, A. Rush.*" The 1850 census of Wakulla County lists only one person as a school teacher. Records indicate that until about 1870 the teacher would live with a family and teach their children, as well as the neighbors' children in the home. After the civil war, schools began appearing in areas where several families were living, farming areas, turpentine camps, logging camps and so forth. These school buildings were built by local people with local funds and were usually shared with church and civic organizations. They were located about six miles apart, serving an area within a three mile radius. They were named for a family in the area, a landmark or a local church. Teachers were also from the local area and were not necessarily well educated. They had to pass a State test on the basics, which included writing, reading, spelling and arithmetic. After passing the test they were given a teaching certificate like Miss Mollie Hall's shown on page 89. Books were furnished by the parents of students and were handed down from generation to generation. One of the best-known books was The Blue Back Speller, which sold for 25 cents in 1870. This book not only covered the spelling and pronunciation of words, but also taught such things as: "*Noah and his family outlived all the people who lived before the flood.*" "*Good manners are always becoming. Ill manners are evidence of low breeding.*" "*A man who saves the fragments of time will accomplish a great deal in his life.*" "*The love of whiskey has brought many a strong fellow to a disgraceful death.*" "*Experience keeps a dear school, but fools will learn in no other.*" These sentences were used to teach the use of words, but I'm sure were also used to lead children in the way they should live. The school term at these rural schools was only three months during the winter, but was lengthened to eight months soon after the turn of the century. By the turn of the century, the area was becoming more populated. People were moving away from the rural areas and the need for higher education was realized.

Following is a description of the Pin Hook School by the author's mother, Jessie French Gerrell, a pupil there from 1916-1920. "*The school building was a one room building about 20 feet by 40 feet. The foundation was sections of logs cut from fat lighter pine, about 24 inches in diameter and 36 inches long. These blocks were stood on end, about ten feet apart and a hewn sill of ten by ten inches of fat lighter was placed on them. Rough sawmill cut two by eights were used for the floor joist, with a one inch pine board of various widths laid for the floor. From this floor, the four outside walls ten feet high went up. The exterior walls were of board and batten style. The roof was made of split cypress shingles. The door and the window shutters were made of the same material as the siding. The building's interior was not sealed, walls nor ceiling, rough rafters, studs, exterior wall boards and shingles could be seen from the inside. The building had tables and benches for the students, with a chair and podium for the teacher. Lunch usually consisted of biscuits, bacon and greens, which was brought to the school in a metal syrup bucket. Syrup was usually left at school in a gallon bucket and could be found near the* old potbellied heater in the center of the room. The syrup, shared by all, was placed near the heater so it would stay warm and pour easily. A water bucket and dipper for everyone's use was by the door. Water came from a nearby spring. There was a time for recreation with games such as skip to my Lou, sugar lump, coffee grows on white oak trees, and King William was David's son.

The local church was making a drive for funds. Two sisters were bearing down hard on old Uncle Rustus. "I can't give nothin'," explained the old man, "I owe nearly everybody in this here town already." "But," said one of the collectors, "don't you think you owe the Lord something, too?" "I does, sister, indeed I does," said the old man, "but he ain't pushing me like all my other creditors is."

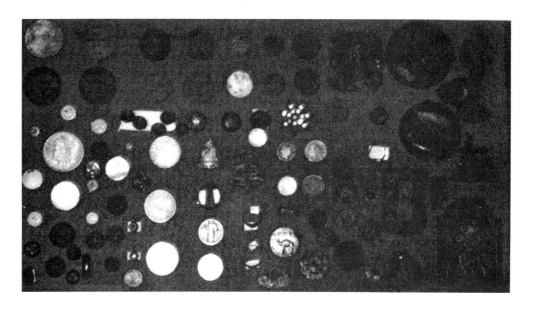

Various coins, buttons and other small items excavated from around camp sites. Items date from 1818 to 1940. (A)

Pigs Feet

Place the pigs feet in hot coals with the hooves against the coals. When they are real hot, the hooves can be sliced out and the meat easily taken off and scraped clean. Then singe the hair off the meat and put them in a pot of salt water and cook them. Or, they can be roasted. Cook until the meat slips off the hoof. They are also good pickled (see the pickling recipe.)

A tourist passing by stops and asks an old fellow "How's times?" "Oh, pretty tolerable," responded the old man who was sitting on a stump. "I had some trees to cut down but a tornado came along and saved me the trouble." "That's fine." "Yeah, and then the lightning set fire to the brush pile and saved me the trouble of burning it." "Remarkable, what are you doing now?" "Oh nothing much, just sitting around waiting for an earthquake to come along and shake the potatoes out of the ground."

Teacher's Certificate.

THIRD CLASS.

OFFICE OF

Board Public Instruction *Wakulla* County,

Dec 7th, 189*1*

This is to Certify, That *Miss Mollie Hall*

of *Wakulla* , having placed on file in the office of the County

Superintendent of Schools of this County satisfactory evidence of maintaining a good moral

character, and having sustained an examination by *The Board of Public*

Instruction

in Reading, Spelling, Writing, Practical Arithmetic, Geography, History of the United States, as

well as in the arts of imparting instruction and managing a School, is therefore entitled to re-

ceive this

Teacher's Certificate of the Third Class,

and is hereby pronounced competent to teach the Public School No. *26* at

Pin Hook , in this County, or such other School as the Board may

direct, until the *Seventh* day of *Dec* , 189*2*, and will be

respected accordingly.

(SIGNED)

W. H. Walker

Chnm Board Public Inst

N. B.—Boards of Public Instruction will issue no Certificates to Applicants who fail to answer eighty per cent. of the
questions submitted on examination.

The author's grandmother's teaching
certificate from Pin Hook School, Wakulla
County, Florida Board of Public Instruction.
(A)

89

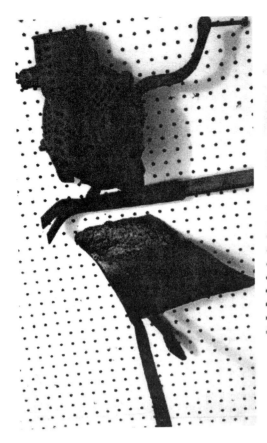

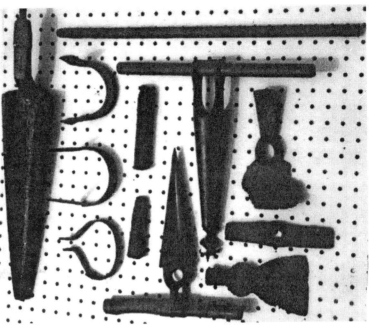

Corn sheller usually mounted on the side of a box to catch the shelled corn as it came off the cob. This one was excavated from a turpentine campsite and the box obviously had rotted away. b. Sugar cane stripper used to strip the fodder off cane before it was carried to the cane mill to have the juice squeezed out of it for making syrup. 41c Hand forged turn plow excavated from a camp site. This turn plow was probably used for farming and cutting firebreaks in the woods. Notice how the blade has been resharpened many times. (A)

Three augers used for either cutting the hole in the center of a wagon hub or for cutting bung holes in barrels. Three scorps used for scraping out the inside of a barrel. Upper right is a foot adze. Below it is a hand forged chisel or hatchet that was obviously mounted on a handle. Bottom right is a hatchet/hammer combination. Items were excavated from turpentine camp sites. (A)

Grits with Fish

Cook grits with cheese mixed, pour in a little sweet milk and let it cook a few minutes just before it's served to make it good and creamy. Take the hot grease with the fried meal in it off the top of the fish grease and pour it over your grits for seasoning.

Indian Breakfast Patties

Pour boiling water on one pint of Indian meal, add one egg and a little salt. Mix thoroughly and fry brown in pork fat. Cut open and put butter on them and serve hot.

Parts of pistols excavated from turpentine camp sites. (A)

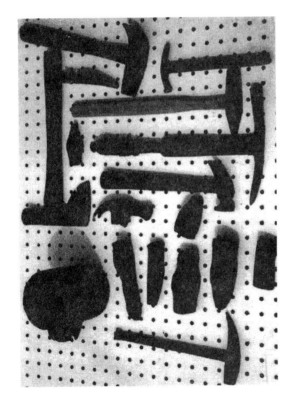

Variety of hammers and hatchets excavated from camp sites. At upper left is a 16 pound sledge hammer used in the building of railroads. (A)

This old hand didn't answer his notice that came from the draft board. The man from the draft board went to check on him and get him during the first part of the Second World War. He got there and said "You didn't answer your draft notice." The old hand said "What's that?" "You're supposed to be in the Army." "What Army?" "Our Army, the American Army," the fellow told him, "We're fighting a war" "Yeah, who we fighting?" "Germany" "Never heered of it. Where's it at?" " Across the ocean." " Then what we fighting them for?" " There's a fellow called Hitler over there who wants to rule the world." "Then why don't somebody shoot him?" "Why you can't even see him, how can you shoot him?" "How come?" " He's in an armored car and he has got a guard of soldiers around everywhere he goes. You just can't get a chance to shoot him." The old hand thought for a few minutes. And then he said, "But he got to come out on the porch and pee sometime, don't he?"

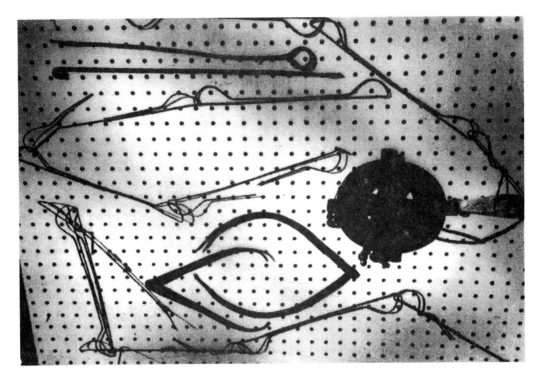

Excavated surveyor's chain and two chaining pins. Newer model surveyor's chain that came into use about 1915. Two sets of hand forged calipers. Items were excavated from a camp blacksmith's shop except for the newer surveyor's chain. (A)

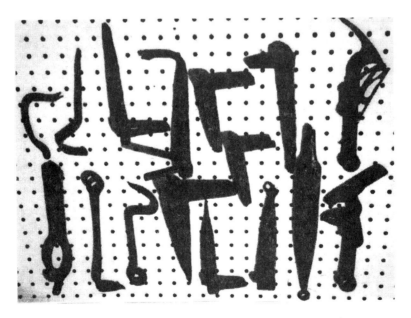

Door and gate hinges and latches excavated from turpentine camp sites. (A)

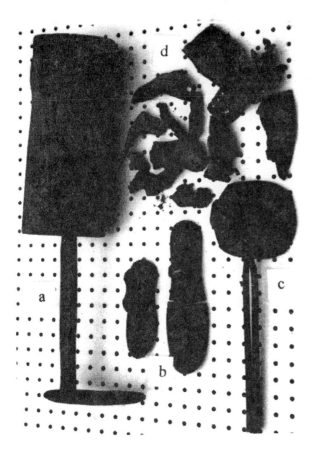

Hand forged "last" used in the making of shoes. b. Two shoe lasts used in the making of shoes. c. Hand forged anvil. d. Pieces of leather shoes. All were excavated from around camp sites. (A)

"My dear wife, I have taken you safely over all the rough places in life, haven't I?" "Yes, I don't believe you missed any of them."

They were taking this old fellow up to boot hill to bury him, but it turned out he wasn't quite dead. Just before he got to the top of the hill the coffin slid off the back of the wagon. It rolled down the hill and rolled back into the town. It happened to roll up into the drugstore. It stood up on end in the drug store and the door opened on it. The druggist looked at the man in the coffin real startled and said, "Can I help you, sir?" The fellow in the coffin said, "Yeah, if you've got something that will stop this coffin."

Excavated items that were probably used in the cooper's shop all are hand forged from old used files. (A)

Flour Gravy

Make the same way as corn meal gravy except don't toast the flour.

Pork Cake

Take one pound of salt pork, chopped fine. Boil a few minutes in 1/2 pint of water. Add 1 cup syrup, 2 cups sugar, 3 eggs, 2 teaspoons of soda, cinnamon, cloves and nutmeg to taste, 1 pound of raisins chopped fine, flour to make a stiff batter. Bake.

Pear Custard

Peel and core the pears. Put them in a deep dish with a small piece of butter, one teaspoon of sugar and a little nutmeg. In the opening of each pear, pour in enough water to cook them. When soft, cool them and cover them with an unbaked custard. Bake until the custard is done.

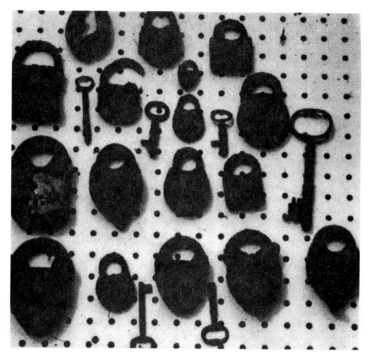

Locks and keys excavated from camp sites.
(A)

Pliers of different descriptions, most of which were excavated from the turpentine camp sites. Some are hand forged. (A)

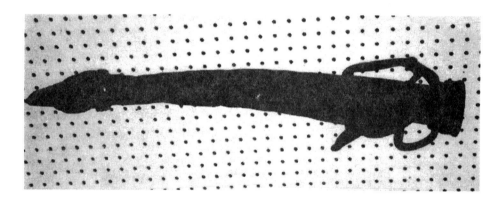

Filler nozzle for "water box" on steam locomotive, excavated from turpentine still site. (A)

Sweet Potatoes

Bake in a medium oven until done through and through. Stick them with a fork to tell when they are done. Serve them hot with the peelings on. Each person will peel their own. Be sure there is plenty of butter on the table. When you peel and slice them, put butter on both sides and go at it.

The doctor of a small country village had two children, the prettiest little girls in the district. While they were out walking one day, they happened to pass two small boys, one of whom was a visitor in the village. Said the latter to his friend, "Who are those pretty little girls?" The village boy replied, "They are the doctor's children. He always keeps the best ones for himself."

The old turpentine hand was riding his bicycle to town after he got paid on Saturday afternoon and The Man comes by in his new Cadillac and asked him if he wanted a ride. "Yes, boss, I'd like to ride, but what am I going to do with my bicycle?" "Well, you can't put it in my car, you might skin my new car up with that old bicycle. But," he said, " I got a rope. Let's just tie your bicycle behind and you can ride it into town with it tied behind me." So he got on his bicycle and The Man got in his car and they started going down the road. The turpentine hand had a whistle in his mouth so that he could whistle if The Man got to going too fast or if he needed to stop for some reason. The Man had already had two or three drinks and somebody came up beside him in a new Lincoln. The fellow revved up his engine in that Lincoln and acted like he wanted to race. So they took off racing and the old turpentine hand hung on the back of the car as it was going faster and faster. There was a Deputy Sheriff sitting by a sign up the road and he saw the two cars racing. He called in and told the dispatcher that there was a Lincoln and a Cadillac racing out here on the road. I think we need to stop them, they're going too fast. He called back in a minute later and said, "Wait a minute, there's an old turpentine hand on a bicycle blowing a whistle trying to pass both of them."

Speaking of navels, I was talking to this old hand in the woods one day and he wanted to know where my older boy that had rode the woods with me before had gone. I said, "Oh, he went off to school." "He did? What's he gonna be?" "Well, he's going to be a naval doctor." "Man, they sho' is specializing these days, ain't they?"

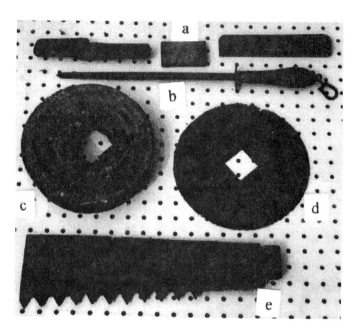

a Whetstones for sharpening knives and "bills", hacks, pulls and scrape irons. b Steel used for sharpening knives. c Whetstone used for sharpening axes. d Metal cutting blade used on the foot operated stand that the whetstone was mounted on. e Part of a hand forged cross-cut saw. (A)

Salt Water Taffy

Take a pound and a quarter of sugar, a pound and a quarter of cane syrup, 2 cups of water, a tablespoon of butter, 2 teaspoons of salt, 1/2 teaspoon of flavoring such as peppermint (use your imagination) and food coloring if you want (not necessary.) Put the sugar, syrup and water in a saucepan and stir it until boiling begins. Continue boiling, but don't stir until it will spin a thread. Take it from the fire and add butter and salt. Pour into buttered platters. When it is cool enough, pull it. Add your flavoring and coloring while you are pulling it. Cut it into pieces, wrap in waxed paper and eat it later.

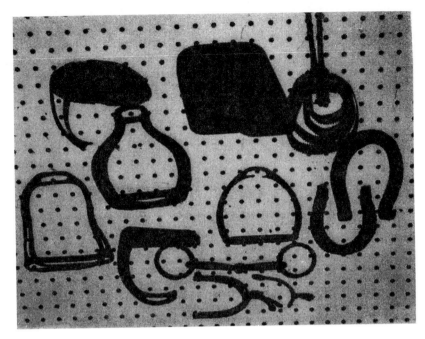

Items excavated from turpentine camp sites. Horseshoes, metal stirrups, spurs and a set of mule bits. Top right is a curry comb without a handle and top center is a cow bell. (A)

A social worker went into one of the houses in a turpentine camp. The housewife was holding a child who was crying lustily, interrupting the conversation continually. Said the social worker, "My dear woman, that child is spoiled." "No, indeedy," said the housewife, "all my kids smell that way."

A man traveling along the road saw a fellow out in a cultivated field, sitting on a stump with a fishing pole, fishing. He stopped at the next house. There was a fellow sitting on the front porch so he asked him "Do you know anything about that fellow out in that cultivated field fishing?" "Sure I do, that's my brother. He ain't quite right, but don't you worry none about him mister, before dark I'm going to crank up the boat and motor and run down there and get him"

Frosting

One cup of sugar and 2 tablespoons of water boiled together. Take it off the stove and stir in the white of one egg, beaten to a stiff froth. Stir all together well, then frost your cake with it. Care should be taken not to let this get on your head or your tongue will slap your brains out trying to git to it.

Peanut Brittle

Take three cups of sugar, a teaspoon of vinegar, a cup of peanuts. Melt the sugar in a pan with the vinegar. When it is melted add the peanuts and stir as little as possible. Pour it onto a buttered platter. Break it up when it is cold.

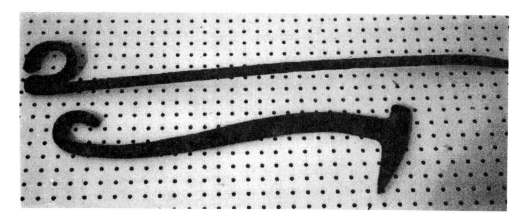

One of a set of three pieces that were used to form a hanger for pots over an open fire. Two of these were driven into the ground and a steel bar placed through the loop in them to suspend pots from. b. Unidentified item that was excavated from a turpentine camp, probably a log pull which was driven into a log with a chain hooked to the hoop end to pull the log with. (A)

Sweet Potato Pie

3 cups of mashed sweet potatoes
1 Tablespoon of butter
1 teaspoon of cinnamon
1/4 cup of cream
1/4 teaspoon of nutmeg
1 cup of sugar
1 pre-baked pie shell
Add the spices and the sugar to the sweet potatoes. Mix together the butter and the cream and stir it into the sweet potato mixture. Pour into a baked pie shell and bake in a medium oven.

Gator

We only ate the young gators (less than 4 feet long.) The meat from older gators was too strong and was only good for dog food. The legs could be skinned and cooked the same as turtle. The tail was skinned, the meat cut cross grain then fried the same as fish. Several meals could be cooked from a four foot gator.

For snakebite, take one onion, a teaspoon of salt, and a teaspoon of turpentine. Cut the onion up very fine and mix it with the salt and turpentine. Apply it to the wound if you're still alive at that time.

"Now Charles," said the teacher, "if your father can do a piece of work in one hour and your mother can do it in one hour, how long would it take both of them to do the same work?" "Three hours," answered Charles, "counting the time they would waste arguing about it."

For sores that break out on you during the Fall of the year, take cane syrup, sulfur and turpentine and mix it into a pill. Take one each night.

(From <u>Florida for Tourists, Invalids and Settlers</u> by Geo. M. Barbour) (FTIS)

They were a strange set of beings. The pleasure-seeker who visits a minstrel entertainment in the North may suppose he is seeing a comical creature of the imagination, but it is not so; in fact, the most grotesque acting or the most distorted lingual expressions that the "nigger delineator" ever perpetrated on the stage is far from equaling the reality as seen and heard in a camp of negro laborers. Such wonderful jokes, such crushing retorts, such verbal pyrotechnics, and such uproarious shouts of laughter, can never be heard elsewhere; and the accompanying gestures and pantomime are often more original and characteristic than the language itself. The only drawback to the amusement of listening at these gatherings is the shocking profanity and disgustingly vile language in which the negroes indulge. The most simple remarks in their social conversation are commonly interlarded with a number of oaths and foul words that is positively startling. They seem to think that it strengthens and emphasizes their conversation; and there can be no doubt that the practice is partly due to their association with low whites, and to a desire to "talk as big as the white folks."

The camp reached, after day's labor, all hands would speedily bring out their stowed-away "grub -boxes." Fires were quickly burning, and soon a multitude of skillets were ranged over the coals, in each a chunk of fat side-pork; this, and a cupful of boiled "grits" or hominy, with molasses for sauce, and a cup of coffee, is their usual meal. Sometimes they vary this with a can of salmon, or a fresh fish caught in the innumerable lakes, or a gopher caught in the woods and made into soup. (This last is a species of large land-turtle ten to twenty

inches across its back-shell, living in deep holes which it burrows in the ground. They are very plentiful, and their cavernous-looking retreats are everywhere seen here. They are incorrectly called "gophers" by the negroes and natives.) They also frequently make up batches of corn or wheat-flour cake, to be eaten with molasses. Pork, however, is their chief article of food; they ate it three times a day, and averaged about five pounds in each seven days.

Meals over, the fun began. Musical instruments, consisting mainly of banjoes, fiddles, and guitars, began thrumming everywhere; soon a jig would strike up, all the feet (such feet!) would begin beating time, and before very long some dancer would bound forward and commence a shuffle, perhaps two or three others joining in, and keep it up until they dropped from sheer exhaustion. And the singing, especially after sunset, was always a noticeable feature, frequently quite fine. When two or three voices start - joined in one of their countless melodies, like nothing heard elsewhere - it is very attractive. Generally all hands in camp would join in the chorus; and when heard a little distance off through the pine-woods, it was strangely beautiful and often solemnly sweet.

As a class, the genuine, pure blacks are always the best laborers; they work hardest, most willingly, honestly and efficiently, always performing the most labor in a day, and making least trouble to the foremen and officers. The genuine African is an excellent, worthy worker. But it is different with "them yeller fellers." These are always more dainty, more quarrelsome; they are the class that carry watches and revolvers, always shirk, always do things a trifle different from the way ordered, always quarrel with their foremen about their time,

99

about their rations, about their pay, and about everything. They are up to all manner of tricks, giving their names differently to their foremen, the commissary clerk, and the paymaster, creating all sorts of unexpected confusion and disputes, requiring close care and watching, greatly increasing the duties of the overseers. If there was any mischief or deviltry in the camp, we nearly always discovered that a mulatto was at the bottom of it.

The 10th of each month was pay-day, the great day with darkeys, and a busy day at the pay-table. It was a regulation holiday with the gangs; not a bit of work would they perform, but at an early hour they would gather at the pay-office - scuffling, dancing, shouting, singing- a happy crowd indeed. One dollar per day was the regular standard price; the colored "spikers" (men who drive the track-spikes) and sub-foremen received a dollar and twenty-five to a dollar and forty cents per day. The older darkeys of about forty or fifty years, especially the genuine blacks, were, as I have said, by far the best laborers; they usually kept records to "tallies" of their labor, and always were correct. But the young darkeys' especially the "yeller fellers," the class that loves to dance and sing, never averaged over fifteen days' labor in the month, and were always disputing their time-accounts.

After pay-day they would strangely be missing - that is, the younger class - but a hunt through the woods would reveal their whereabouts; under the trees and in out-of-the-way thickets they were to be found in small, quiet, earnest-faced little groups - gambling! The darkey is a most inveterate gambler, the equal of the Chinaman or Indian in this vice. The Chinaman will gamble himself away - that is, he will bind himself to work for his winning opponent for

certain lengths of time; the Indian will gamble away his horses, tepees (or wigwams), squaws, and papooses; but the darkey will gamble all he has earned by months of hard labor, and all he can steal from his hard-working fellow-laborers.

After two or three days, the gangs would begin to return to work, silent for a day or two, dispirited, disgusted, dead-broke - in fact, "played out."

Two or three of them wouldn't return to work - no, sir!. They put on airs, joked, smoked cigars, ate melons, bananas, etc, and went on a trip down the river to Jacksonville, bought watches, canes, etc. They were the winning gamblers.

The pay-rolls exhibited a lamentable condition of ignorance among them, less than ten per cent, signing their names. About thirty or forty whites of the poorer class of natives were employed on the gangs, and the lack of education was even greater among this class, for less than four percent could sign their names. In reply to the request to "sign your name," the old darkeys always politely replied, "I can't write, sir" ; but the whites would, in a shamed manner and low tone, say "You jest put it down, please, my hand is hurted and sort o' weak like - ahem!" or they would remark that their hand was "so dirty." I have seen them slyly wrap a bit of cloth or a handkerchief about their hand while awaiting their turn, so as have an excuse for not signing.

As a rule, the young blacks can read and write, and are very proud of the accomplishment. They seize the pen and delight to attach their autographs (generally of three or four names, the Williams and Johnsons greatly in the majority) in an airy, rapid, careless sort of style; it always profoundly impresses the assembled lookers-on, and adds a dignity to the labor that is quite overpowering to witness. The blacks are always solid friends to all educational improvements. In all their camps were individuals who did the reading and writing; read the newspapers aloud, read the letters received by their less intelligent companions, and wrote the letter and postal-card replies - this class are "immense" on letters. Frequently these scribes (always young) make a pretty good thing of it in this amanuensis service.

It was often a group quite worth seeing to visit one of their camps in the evening. There the large fire of pitch-pine knots was blazing brightly, lighting up their small collection of queer little huts built of railroad-ties, in the tall pine-woods, making a good picture indeed, with the entire party all grouped about one of their number - all intently listening to him reading the latest newspaper; they always insisted that he should read it all. Such intense attention, eager eyes, and various attitudes, such quiet, earnest facial expressions, and such costumes - or lack of costumes - all frequently formed pictures that would delight an artist.

And after the reading was completed, then to hear the Babel of arguments, opinions, and comicalities, was another source of interest to the observer. Often their jokes and puns were quite original and good.

It is always something of an astonishment to find how well posted these otherwise ignorant negroes are on political matters, local events, or any important occurrences; they seem to have a secret sort of freemasonry by which they learn everything going on. Ignorant, but very cunning and unscrupulous, they would be a terribly dangerous element of society, were it not for their well-known fear of fire-arms, and their naturally peaceful disposition. As a rule, all negroes go armed; razors are their characteristic and specially favorite weapon; but they are very fond of revolvers also, and many of them carry one. Give the ordinary negro a cheap shiny watch, a revolver, and a cane, and he is "happy as a lord."

101

● 08359

Sopchoppy, Florida, *1-27*   19*48*

Sold To. *Wakulla Turp. Co.*

Address

QUAN.	DESCRIPTION	PRICE	AMOUNT
1/2	cs 24/1 1/2 Kans - Red Label		2	35
4	25 Pillsbury S.R.		9	20
1	Bu 5/10 Talla Meal		3	35
1	" 10/5 " "		3	40
1	" 20/3 W. M. Rice		8	90
1/2	cs 100/1/4 Flat Sardine		6	13
1	" 24/2 Tomatoes		3	25
2	Dz 14 Matches		1	90
1/2	cs 12 oz Soda		1	00
			39	48

1948 Receipt for items to be resold in the commissary. (WT)

KAESER & BLAIR, INC., CINCINNATI, OHIO —52652△

An old hand being examined by a liberal: "If you had a million dollars would you give half of it to the State?" "Sure, I would." "If you had a thousand acres of land, would you give half of it to the State?" "Sure, I would." "If you had two pigs, would you give one of them to the State?" "No!" "Why not?" "Well, I got two pigs."

"Now," she asked, "is there any man in the audience who would let his wife be slandered and say nothing. If so, stand up." A meek little man rose to his feet. The lecturer glared at him. "Do you mean to say you would let your wife be slandered and say nothing?" she cried. "Oh, I'm sorry," he apologized, "I thought you said slaughtered."

East Point, Fla. Feb. 24/193_

Mess. Wakulla Turpentine Co.
Wakulla Fla
Gentlemen

Some time ago wrote you regards to a negro, Amos Allen, which we understood was at your place, this negro is due us $20.40 which we are due you for some Cup which we have been able to pay if he is with you Cant you Credit our acct with this amt and Charge him with same. Let us know if this is all right and we will Mail you a receipt for this amt if he is not with you will you please Let me know eny of his whereabout.

Yours Truly
Morrison Turpentine Co.
By Jas. H. Morrison

<table>
<tr><td>For boils and pimples, take a handful of balm of Gilead buds and 1/2 pint of hog's lard, 1 tsp of sulfur, 1 tsp of spirits of turpentine. Fry them all together and apply when you go to bed.</td><td>For boils, take a piece of gum camphor the size of a hickory nut. Dissolve it in an ounce of turpentine. Bind a cloth around the boil. Keep the cloth wet all the time with the turpentine and camphor mixture.</td></tr>
</table>

103

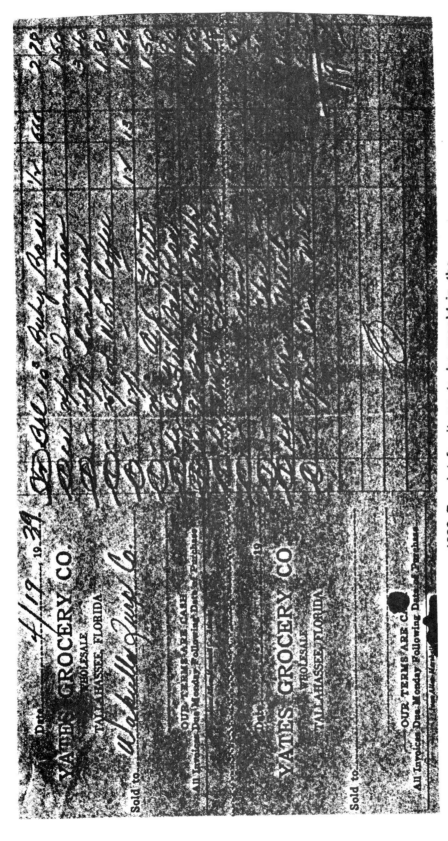

1939 Receipt for items to be resold in the commissary. The first item on this list as well as others I've researched was 1/2 barrel of wine for the high price of $2.78. This was probably the only legal alcoholic beverage available to the hands. There was always someone that had a "still" located near the camp, which was a smaller version of the turpentine still, that was used to make "moonshine." (WT)

104

J. R. D. LASTER & COMPANY
UNDERTAKERS AND FUNERAL DIRECTORS
ALL ROBES AND FUNERAL EQUIPMENT FURNISHED

PHONE 333 BOTH LONG AND SHORT DISTANCE   27 WEST PENSACOLA STREET

TALLAHASSEE, FLORIDA Dec 1 1930

Mr W. C. Culbert,
Wakulla Fla,
     Dear Sir½-
    allow me to ask a favor of you, you have a man working for you by Name of Lenard Austine,
this man Lenard Austine wife died Jan 4 1929 this woman was name Adline Austine,
the Balance due on the Funeral expence is $ 48,75 see if you can get this man to pay a part
of this account each month out of his wages,

               Your Truly

               J. R. D. Laster

Eel Stew

Take from three to four pounds of eels and clean thoroughly inside and out, removing the heads and tails from the bodies. Cut them into pieces three inches long and lay them in a stew pan. Cover them with sweet mutton gravy and keep them simmering over a slow open fire. When they have cooked for twenty minutes, add a quarter of an ounce of whole black pepper, a quarter of an ounce of allspice, with one or two pieces of white ginger to the liquor before you place your eels into it . Thicken with a light mixture of flour and butter, stirring it around, adding at the same time, one gill of good port wine and 1/2 gill of sweet ketchup. (Eels were often caught on bush hooks and trot lines set in the rivers and sinkholes on weekend nights.)

A preacher was driving back to town from one of the camps on Sunday, when he came upon an old hand with a club in one hand and a freshly killed possum in the other. The preacher stopped to examine the prize and said, "My friend, do you know it's Sunday?" "Yes, sir, Boss." "Are you not a religious man?" "I are. I was just on my way home from church." "And what sort of religion have you got that permits you to go huntin' on Sunday?" "Religion?" inquired the man as he held the possum up with one hand and scratched his head with the other, "You 'spect any old hand in Florida is going to tie himself up to any religion that allows a possum to walk right across the road ahead of him and get away free? No sir, a religion which won't bend a little when a fat possum heads you off couldn't be established around here by all the preachers in the universe."

TURPENTINE STILL

When an operator acquired six crops of trees in an area it was economical for him to locate a still nearby. Some of the factors that were important in the location and operation of a still were: yields and grades of turpentine and rosin available; construction of a still building; cost of maintenance; costs of hauling; labor costs; fire risks; the existing and potential timber supply; water supply and storage and shipping facilities.

The size and design of the still was considered. Probably the most important and most difficult step in the erection of a fire still was the selection of a site. Among the many points to be considered were 1) the lay of the land, which would determine the type of ramp, drainage system and rosin handling facilities, 2) the layout of the plant that would provide the most efficient location of each building and storage space for raw materials, 3) size of storage area to be used for turpentine and rosin, and 4) fire risks. From forty to fifty acres of land were necessary for the still and its supporting facilities consisting of office, commissary, still building, rosin cooling shed, cooper's shop, stillers' and hands' quarters, turpentine storage areas, garage, stable and at least a 2000 barrel rosin yard.

For the topography of the still site, if possible sloping ground was selected for the still building in order to take advantage of gravity in handling of the crude gum and the finished products. The still building was located so that the gum could be offloaded directly from the truck to the still platform. If the ground had a slope of from 8 to 12 feet per hundred feet, a gravity flow still could be used. With such a still site, rosin could run directly into the barrels from the end of the rosin vat. For ease of handling,

the full barrels, rosin and turpentine should move downhill to their respective storage areas. The rosin yard should be a well-drained area, at least 100 feet from the nearest building. An ample supply of cold water for the cooling tub, preferably below 70 degrees Fahrenheit was required for efficient condensation of the spirits. The water used in the kettle must be clear and colorless to avoid contamination of the rosin with foreign matter. The less dissolved mineral matter there was in the kettle water the better. Iron compounds in the water and rust, particularly, were injurious as even extremely small quantities of iron would darken the color and lower the grade of rosin. Water from shallow wells generally was soft and more suitable for kettle use than water from deep or artesian wells. A suitable drinking water supply was necessary with wells located and protected so that the water would not be contaminated by surface drainage.

Adequate facilities for shipping the turpentine and rosin were considered, with the still being located on a railroad or arterial highway if possible.

After the site had been selected, the next step was the location of buildings on the site. Most important was the still building, which should be placed on sloping, well-drained, dry ground. The still building should be large enough to provide the deck floor space needed for the handling and storage of gum received and to permit the sorting of the gum by classes. Sorting enabled the stiller to group the still charges that would produce a grade of rosin yielding the highest monetary return. The rosin vat was to be large enough and placed so as to prevent rain water from getting into the vat or barrels after the rosin had been strained and dipped. A stable for livestock and a garage should be at least 100 feet from all other buildings and on the leeward side of prevailing winds. Protection from weather for both live and rolling stock was necessary. The commissary and office were usually in the same building, but should be in separate rooms.

At stills located on level ground the hands would roll the dip barrels, each weighing about 500 pounds, up a wooden ramp to the second level, where they were placed for emptying into the copper kettle. Some stills had a dirt or log ramp alongside the still building so the hands could offload the barrels directly onto the second level.

Charging the still: After the barrels had been brought up the ramp, they were emptied into the top of the copper kettle. This operation was called charging. When the kettle was filled to the gum line, the cap was placed, tightened securely, then the fire started. The temperature was brought up to and maintained at about 190 degrees Fahrenheit for about two hours, until the charge was cooked. As soon as the charge finished cooking, the kettle was uncapped and allowed to cool until it stopped frothing. Then the tailgate was opened and the hot rosin drawn off and strained. About four charges would usually be processed in a day.

In the foreground is the platform where barrels of gum were offloaded when they were brought in from the woods. The log ramp was used to roll the 500 pound barrels of gum up to the second level of the still. (Mc)

For a sore throat, mix pine tar with hog lard and put it on a flannel cloth. Tie it around your neck.

Left is a side view of the strainers that are over the rosin vat, outside the still's tailgate. Right is the cooling tub and separating barrels. (GA)

Condensing coil and tub (tank): As a charge cooked, the turpentine and water vapors were forced through an outlet in the top of the kettle to the condensing coils. These ran through a cypress wood tank of cool water that condensed the vapor inside the coil and then emptied the resulting liquid into the first separator barrel. Water for the tank was maintained at about 70 degrees Fahrenheit, with water pumped in from shallow wells or a nearby river as necessary.

Separating barrels: In the first separating barrel the spirits of turpentine, being lighter than water, would rise to the top. Most of the water settled to the bottom. A siphon pipe located just below the rim of the first barrel drained the turpentine into the second separating barrel, called a dehydrator. There, it filtered through rock salt which extracted the remaining water. It was very important that all water be removed from the turpentine. Water not extracted could cause leaks to develop in wooden barrels, or rust discoloration to develop in metal containers. A drain plug at the bottom of the first barrel allowed water or "low wine" to drain off.

A boy applied for a job in a butcher shop. "How much will you give me?" "Three dollars a week, but what can you do to make yourself useful around a butcher shop?" "Anything." "Well, be specific, can you dress a chicken?" "Not on three dollars a week, I can't"

"Do you object to petting?" "That's one thing I've never done yet." "You mean you never petted?" "No, objected."

View of both levels of the still with a dip
wagon under the second level, also shown

on the second level are the resin (gum)
barrels in place for charging the still. (GA)

CARSON NAVAL STORES COMPANY

FACTORS AND WHOLESALE GROCERS
GRAHAM BUILDING

JACKSONVILLE, FLORIDA

August 15th, 1930

Wakulla Turpentine Company
Wakulla, Florida

Dear Sirs:

Your letter of the 14th ordering 1 dozen D. E. Scrape Irons
has been received and noted, and we are shipping these to you today,
at Wakulla, Florida, by express.

Thanking you, and with kind regards and best wishes, we remain,

Yours very truly,

CARSON NAVAL STORES COMPANY

BY _Thomas M. Kill._

MANAGER

109

The opening in the top of kettle where the charge is placed (the raw gum is poured) on the second level of the still. About ten barrels of raw gum, which made a charge, were emptied into the copper kettle along with water. It was cooked at 190 degrees for about two hours. (GA)

Cane Syrup Cookies

1/2 cup of butter
1/2 tsp of cinnamon
1/2 cup of sugar
1/2 tsp of ginger
1 egg
1/4 tsp cloves
1/4 cup of syrup
2 cups of unsifted flour
1/4 tsp of baking soda
dash of salt

Cream the butter and sugar together. Add eggs and syrup. Stir together the dry ingredients and blend into the creamed mixture. Roll out and cut it with a cookie cutter. Bake in a medium oven until done, about 8 minutes.

View of the turpentine still. The collector barrel is in building to the left. In the foreground is the firebox and chimney. This type of still, called a fire still, was first used in the industry in 1834 for distilling resin from the pine trees. (Mc)

Rosin strainers and vats: As soon as the still cooled enough that it stopped frothing, the tail gate was opened and the rosin released from the kettle into the strainers. There were three sets of strainers. The first was covered with a 4 by 4 wire mesh. The second was covered with the same 4 by 4 wire mesh for strength, then a very fine mesh of brass wire. The third was covered by the same wire mesh, which was overlaid with cotton. Impurities collected on the coarse strainer were called "dross" and were used to start fires around the camp. Impurities collected on the second strainer were called "straight dross", which was sold as a low grade of rosin. The cotton filter from the bottom strainer was rolled up after it dried and also sold as batting dross (a low grade of rosin.) After filtering through these three strainers, the pure rosin was collected in the V shaped vat under the strainers from which it was dipped into rosin barrels. The quality of rosin was determined by its color, the lighter its shade the higher the grade. Rosin was the most important by-product of the distilling process.

Still tailgate and the first strainer (the coarse wire strainer). A sluice door (tailgate) in the still was opened and the boiling rosin gushed out into the strainers and vat. (GA)

The chips of wood dross strained from the boiling gum by the top strainer were used locally for kindling. (GA)

Aunt Agatha was recovering from an attack of the flu and was upset to have all her well-meaning but tactless visitors tell her how ill she still looked. Her nephew, a sympathetic little lad, was doing his best to comfort her. "Don't you let them make you feel sorry, Auntie," he said, "I don't think you look a bit worse now than you did before."

All three strainers over the vat. The rope tied to the top strainer was used to shake the strainers so the rosin would pour through faster. At the end of the cooking time, about two barrels of spirits of turpentine had been distilled with six or seven barrels of rosin remaining in the bottom of the still to be released and filtered. (GA)

Long handle dippers used to dip the hot rosin out of the vat and into the rosin barrels. The rosin strained into a trough (vat) and while still in a semi-fluid state, was ladled into barrels by means of these long handled dippers. A portion of the hot rosin stuck to the cotton batting. The refuse from the bottom strainer was known as "batting dross" and from the middle strainer as "strainer dross." Especially adapted refineries purchased this dross from which the rosin was recovered. (GA)

Hog Brains

Take the hog brains and put them in hot water and boil them for a minute to loosen the veil of skin covering them. Then add a little salt and pepper to them and boil. When they are cooked you can add them to scrambled eggs.

The hog snout is usually roasted. The heart, liver, and lights or lungs (whichever you prefer to call them) are usually cut up and boiled and made into a stew. Some people even throw the tail and kidneys in as well as possibly the tongue if they don't choose to use it otherwise.

Venison Stew

Cut off the fat of part of a loin of venison and cut into chops. Pare, wash and slice some potatoes, two onions, and two small carrots seasoned with pepper and salt. Cover with water in a stew pot and stew gently until the meat is tender and the potatoes are dissolved in the gravy. It may also be made from beef or venison mixed with beef.

112

Resin (gum) barrels that have been emptied into the still and prepared for sending back to the woods for refilling. (GA)

Rosin barrels at the end of the tail gate and strainers. Note that the barrels were wood with metal rings. They were made so that they could be taken apart when the rosin hardened. After the rosin was sold the barrels would be disassembled and shipped back to the still for another filling. (GA)

A 50 gallon barrel of raw gum after distilled, would yield about eleven gallons of turpentine and 330 to 340 pounds of rosin. A skillful "stiller" cooked off a charge in about two hours without the aide of gauges or thermometers in the earlier years, adjusting the distillation rate by listening through the kettle's tailpipe to the bubbling water and resin mixture. The temperature of the still was controlled by adding or decreasing the amount of wood in the fire box under and around the still kettle and the stiller, listening to the bumping noise within the still, could tell whether to add or decrease wood. He also had a supply of clean water that he could add to the charge if needed.

In the late 1930's the centralized industrial steam distillation plant replaced the fire stills and changed the operation. Rather than stills being located in the woods, they were located in the towns at rail facilities. The still owner usually bought the raw gum from the producers. The price paid to the producer was determined by multiplying the potential number of gallons of turpentine in the barrel by the price per gallon and the number of pounds of rosin in the barrel by the price per 100 pounds of that grade. The sum of these two factors rendered the price per barrel paid to the turpentine farmer, after deducting for the weight (pare) of his empty container.

Tongue (hog, cow or deer)

Clean it by pouring boiling water over it and scraping it. Then boil it in salt water with black pepper until it is tender. Slice it and serve it. This goes good with Spanish Moss Jelly and Fried Mush.

Liberal: You should give me half of all you've got for the government. Old Timer: Well, all right. All I have left is rheumatism and halitosis, which one would you choose?

Before the introduction of the metal barrels in the mid 1930's, turpentine operators employed a barrel maker, "cooper", that made the wooden barrels at the still site. The author's great grandfather Gerrell was a cooper that built barrels from white oak or hickory staves. He would buy a tract of land with hickory or white oak trees on it and cut the trees to build barrels to sell to the turpentine operators. In later years, after the hickory and white oak supply was depleted, some of the coopers began making barrels with pine. The cooper placed staves into temporary wooden forming hoops to get an approximate fit before hooping the cask with permanent metal bands. He inserted a small brazier, fueled by oak shavings, within the circumference of the staves, periodically swabbing the barrel's interior with a water soaked mop, steaming the staves into shape. Using a metal hammer and chisel-like hoop driver, he pinched a metal band down on the barrel while alternately heating and swabbing until the staves took on a familiar mid-bulging contour, narrowed at both ends by forming hoops. At this point, he pared the staves' ends with a croze - a half moon shaped wood planer, cut in grooves to accommodate the barrel head and barrel round, (top and bottom.) As the wood cooled, the cooper removed the forming hooks, inserted the head and round, and hammered on the finishing bands. In completing a spirit barrel, he used a bung auger to drill the filling holes in the side. To make the cask leakproof, he poured several gallons of hot hide glue into the barrel, coating its interior with a rocking motion before draining out the excess glue. Rosin barrels were disassembled, when received by the rosin buyer, and shipped back to the producer. This could be accomplished because the rosin, when cooled, would solidify and retain its barrel-like shape.

Stencil used for labeling the top of the barrels before they were shipped so they could be returned to the owner after the contents were sold. (GA)

Pieces of rosin excavated in 1994 from a turpentine still site. The still was moved in about 1900. This indicates how the rosin lasts for many years, even though it is underground. (A)

Dad: Son, I don't want you going with that wild girl again. Son: Dad, she isn't wild, anyone can pet her.

114

Information taken from the United States Department of Agriculture, miscellaneous production Number 387, Washington D.C., printed by the U.S. Government Printing Office in 1940.

IX. Specifications for an efficient 10 barrel fire still

A. Construct the still masonry in accordance with the approved government style of setting wing wall, outside chimney, 16" or 17" still walls, asbestos sheeting and mortar, fire brick, iron rails over kettle, etc.

B. Preferably the copper kettle should have fixed cap and removable lid.

C. The condensing worm should be a 35 barrel size.

D. The cooling tub should be of cypress 10 feet in diameter and 12 feet high.

E. The water for cooling should be from a deep well or free flowing and as cool as possible.

F. Specifications for low insurance rates or details for greater fire protection:

1. Government style setting as above.

2. A standard make thermometer properly installed, in good condition and used regularly.

3. Fireproof roof on still shed and over gum platform.

4. Metal guard over fire door joining wing wall with outside chimney flue.

5. Tubs of sand and barrels of water on deck and near.

6. Double floor or deck with waterproof paper or tin in between and a 4" wood dam on deck.

7. No smoking signs in prominent places and the rules strictly observed.

8. Turpentine and rosin stored over 100 feet from the still shed.

9. Separator barrel and spirit tub covered.

10. Batting dross, rock dross and chips 50 feet or more from the still. Two barrels may be kept closer, but not nearer than 25 feet from the still.

11. Fire drawn and thoroughly wet before discharge and all skimmings and so forth wet down with water.

12. All buildings more than 75 feet from the still.

X. Distillation

A. Twelve gallons of water or more should be used to cool down the still.

B. A proper charge consists of ten barrels of virgin, yearling or raised cup gum, 9 barrels of gum from faces unraised one year, 8 barrels of old high pulled gum, or from 10 to 12 300 pound barrels of scrape.

C. For proper temperature control for making high grade rosin and for making less batting dross a thermometer is essential.

D. A ten ounce graduated glass will provide a fairly accurate check on distillation.

E. For proper thermometer or graduated glass control the "Turpentine Stilling Chart" should be used as a guide.

F. A mixture of dried heart and old dried sap, not rotted wood, makes the best fuel.

G. Turn out charge with some foam on the rosin.

XI. Separation of turpentine and low wine.

A. A separator barrel should be fitted with automatic drain pipe (1.5" brass) for low wine draining from near the bottom of the barrel and emptying out 1" below the spirit pipe level.

B. A dehydrator filled with salt through which the turpentine must flow should be used. Coarse rock salt or ice cream salt should be used.

C. Both separator barrel and dehydrator should be covered to prevent evaporation of turpentine.

XII. Rosin handling

A. For straining rosin use first strainer - #4 mesh.

Second strainer - #30 mesh on # 4 mesh.

Third strainer - cotton batting on # 4 mesh.

The first strainer 12' x 10" - 11" deep x 33" wide. Second strainer 14' by 10" - 11" deep x 33" wide. The third strainer 16' x 10" - 11" deep x 33" wide. The top of the strainers should be flared.

B. The vat should be constructed of tongue and groove D4S nailed to a 2" x 4" frame with an air space of 4" between outer and inner sides.

C. Pour or dip rosin to cause the least amount of stirring possible.

D. Allow rosin to sit as undisturbed as possible for two to three days after placing it in the barrels.

XIII. Rosin barrel making

A. A barrel drawn up with a ratchet or winch should be made tight without the use of clay.

XIV. Gluing and care of spirit barrels

A. The glue should be melted in a double pot.

B. Borax should be added to eliminate mold in the glue.

C. Glue should be of the proper consistency before applying.

D. After settling overnight, water should be thieved out of barrel.

XV. Night Charging

A. Fire underwriters prohibit night charging of the still.

XVI. Skimming

A. Dip should not need to be skimmed.

B. Scrape can be skimmed when ready for water.

A turpentine still in Wakulla County, FL that was in operation in the mid 1930's. In 1936 in the Deep South about one half million Naval Stores units were produced. A unit consisted of one 50 gallon barrel of turpentine and three and a third 420 pound net barrels of rosin. The annual production amounted to 25 million gallons of turpentine and 490 million pounds of rosin. The entire production for the United States came from a few of the southern states. The percent produced by Georgia was about 60 % and for Florida about 30%. Almost 60% of the world's production of turpentine was from the southern United States. Much of the Naval Stores were produced at what were called turpentine camps. There were about 1000 such camps in the South, with more than 400,000 men engaged in collecting and processing gum. The camps were located conveniently near sufficient timber to support their continuous operation for at least ten years. About six crops of faces were necessary to operate a typical turpentine camp. A crop was comprised of 10,000 turpentine faces. (FDS)

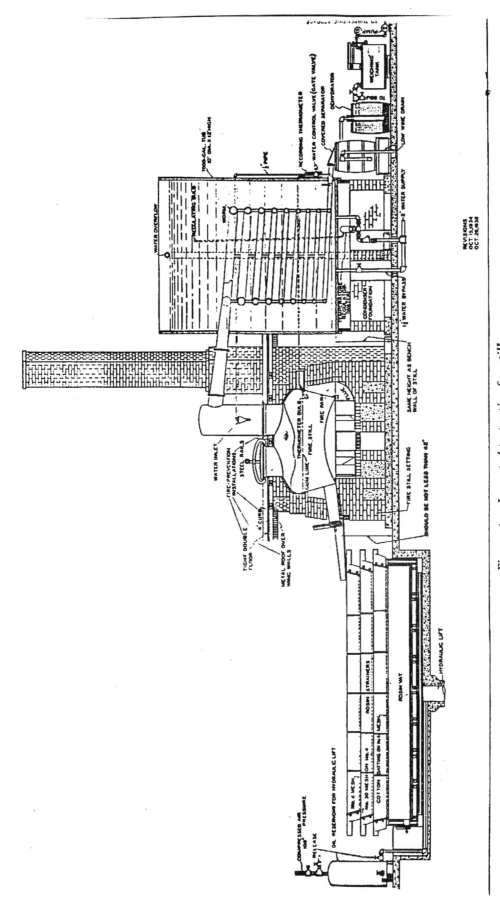

Figure 1.—Layout of turpentine fire still.

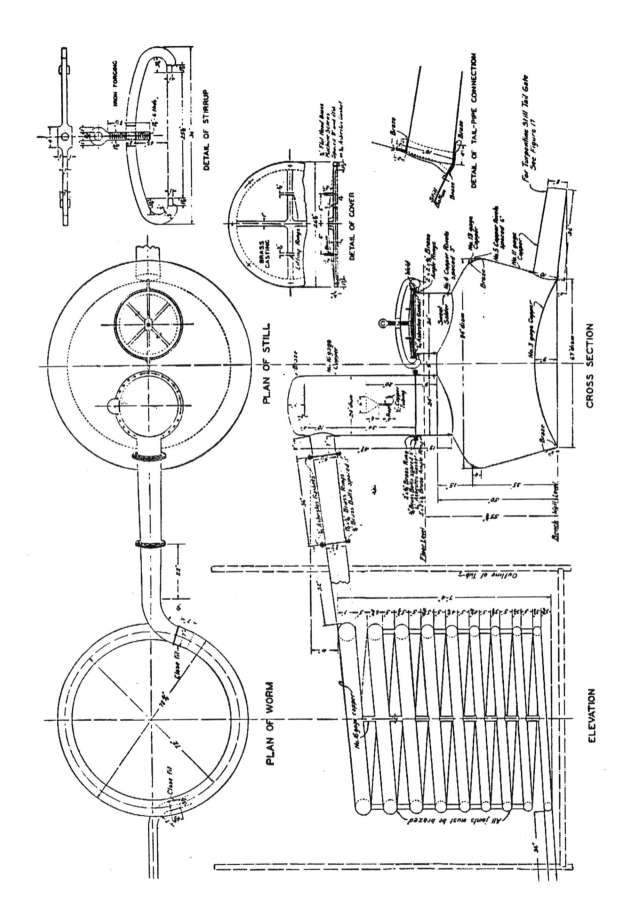

Figure 16.—*Turpentine fire still.*

119

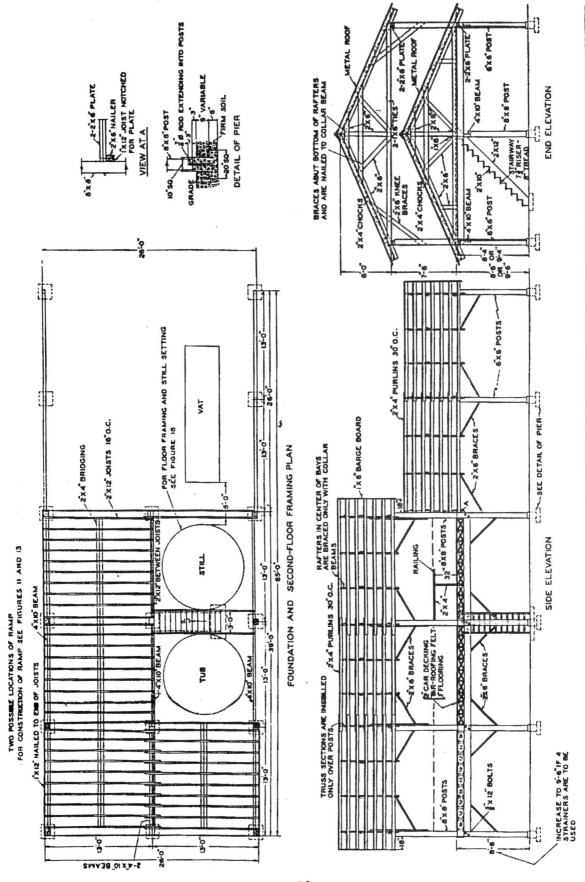

Figure 4.—*Plan A for turpentine still building.*

120

Turpentine ramp alongside the Tallahassee-St. Marks Railroad. This ramp was used to load barrels of turpentine onto a train to be shipped to Valdosta, GA for processing. Note the thousands of metal cups stored upside down on the ramp with metal barrels in the background. This was obviously a later years operation.

121

CHIPLEY STAVE COMPANY

Manufacturers of

CYLINDER SAWN STAVES AND CIRCLED HEADING

S.A.ALFORD

J. H. FAULK

CHIPLEY, FLORIDA

March 11th, 1930.

Wakulla Turpentine Company
Wakulla, Fla.

<u>Att'n Mr. Culbreth.</u>

Gentlemen:-

It has been quite awhile since we have had the pleasure of shipping you any rosin barrels and we have missed this business very much. We are in position to furnish you as good a barrel if not better than ever before at a price of 65¢ per set delivered 817 mile post or any point on St. Marks branch of Seaboard.

At present we are not crozing our barrel but since there seems to be a growing demand for a crozed barrel we have ordered a crozing and champfering machine and should have this machine in operation within a few weeks.

Awaiting with interest your reply, we are,

Yours very truly,

CHIPLEY STAVE COMPANY
By

J. W. Alford

A/A

Fish Balls

Boned, cooked fresh or salt fish. Add double the quantity of mashed potatoes, one beaten egg, a little butter, pepper and salt to the taste. Make it into cakes or balls. Dredge with flour and fry in hot hog lard.

The pastor, examining one of the younger Sunday school classes, asked the question "What are the sins of omission?" After a little silence, one young lady offered, "Please sir, they're sins we out to have committed and haven't."

CARSON NAVAL STORES COMPANY
FACTORS AND WHOLESALE GROCERS

Savannah, Ga.
Feb. 20th, 1930.

Dear Sirs:-

We again remind you that this Corporation maintains a warehouse with a complete line of turpentine distillers' supplies, including all distillers' needs, and tools and equipment for woods work. For your information we touch on the following items:

SPIRIT BARRELS: The barrel factories have all raised prices and are endeavoring to secure a uniform price of $3.15 each f.o.b. plant. It is our idea that this move is untimely and we have placed ourselves in position to fill your orders at a lower figure. We are always in position to meet legitimate competition and when you are in need of barrels we will be glad to have your orders, or we will quote delivered prices on receipt of your inquiry.

COTTON BATTING: Strainer batting will be sold at a lower price than that which prevailed last season. It might be well to call your attention to the fact that 60 pound bales as well as 75 pound bales are on the market and a cheap quotation would very likely indicate that the lighter bale is being offered.

HOOP IRON: Competition from foreign sources is not so keen this year as last, labor prices having advanced in Continental Europe and the selling price of foreign iron has moved up accordingly. We handle only American iron, uniform as to thickness and of the lightest specifications permitted by the trade rules.

GLUES: We are in position to furnish your requirements of glue at a lower price than last season, having made an advantageous contract. We handle only glues which we have thoroly tested and found to be exactly suited to the sizing of spirit barrels. The Turpentine Operator will make no mistake in buying his glue from his Factor. It is to our interest that your turpentine arrive to market in sound barrels and we are too well aware of the trouble incurred thru the use of cheap glues, which in most cases, are not suitable for sizing purposes.

Let us have your inquiries and orders. We will at all times take care of you and at prices consistent with the market and best quality goods.

Yours very truly,

CARSON NAVAL STORES COMPANY

123

WEEKLY DIP REPORT

Scrape Report at Still   11-29-37.

NAME	MON	TUES	WED	THUR	FRI	SAT	TOTAL	AT	AMOUNT
James Broken + Theo Washington	1	3	2	1	3		10		
Sam Boope	1		1	2	1		5		
Bobe Hall	1			2			3		
Will Walker		2		2	2		6		
Harry Johnson		3	3	3			9		
Tom Chatman		1	3		2		6		
Harold Mansfield				2			2		
Harry Hall + Robt Miller				3			Bought Scrape		

On Hand at still 22 dipp
23 Scrape

Crops Dipped This Week

Date 11 29 37 Still Report			MON	TUES	WED	THUR	FRI	SAT	TOTAL	Poured Cups IN CROP	Spell DIP PER M	Batter NO. STREAKS
Hancock	Geo William	2		8				17	13	3	1 Batter
30 ✓ ✓	✓ ✓	2	5	6		•		12	13	3	
1 ✓ ✓	✓ ✓	2	5	1			2	15	12	2	1 Batter
2 ✓ ✓	✓ ✓	2	7	8				7	12	3	1 Batter
3 ✓ ✓	✓ ✓	2	8	10				51	10	3	
		10		33			2		60	14	

REMARKS: WOODSMAN 33   WEEK ENDING

FORM NO. 103 - COPYRIGHT PENDING. TURPENTINE DISTRIBUTING CO

124

HIGH BLUFF TURPENTINE CO.

MANUFACTURERS OF NAVAL STORES

C. C. LAND, MANAGER

Sumatra, Florida

March
March.12, 1934.

Mr B.H. Linslet

Cross City. Fla
Dear Sir,

As you will recall I had to answer to a charge of peonage at Federal court in Tallahassee in January of of this year witch I was successful in securing release form.

One fo thewitnewsses for the goverment was an old negro name Lee Middleton, and recently a goverment agent has advise me that old negro has never xxxxxx returned to South Fla. since leving Tallahassee, were his wife and son live on Mr. J. R. Moody job near Newahotee. Fla.

If you know or can find out anything about his where abouts I will certainly appreciate your advising me since as unless he is found it throw somewhat of a suspicion on me as knowing something about him when honestly I know nothing of him and the last time I saw him was in the Court room in Tallahassee.

Thinking he might stop by and went to work withn you all I am writing ths letter.

Trusting that I shall bee favored with your immediate reply and with best wishes. I am,

Yours very sincerely,

C. C. Land Sumatra. Fla.

A man was carried to court and charged with abusing his team and using loud and profane language. One of the witnesses was an old turpentine hand. "Did the defendant use improper language while he was beating his horses?" asked council. "Well, he talked mighty loud, sir." "Did he indulge in profanity?" The witness seemed puzzled, so the lawyer put the question in another form. "What I mean, Uncle, is did he use words that would be proper for a minister to use in a sermon?" "Oh, yes sir," the man replied with a grin, "but they would have to be arranged in a different order."

Are there any divorces in heaven? Of course not. You can't get a divorce without a lawyer.

Poorlow

When we killed chickens we would give the parts that we didn't want to eat to an old woman that helped. She would take the heads, back and feet. She said that her favorite part was the "foots" because of the soft, sweet-tasting pad on the bottom. The Poorlow was prepared by heating the chicken parts in a pot of water on the wood stove or open fire. When the water started to boil, she would remove the toenails from the foot. After they boiled a few minutes, she would remove the yellow scaly covering from the legs and remove the comb, beak and gullet from the head. After it all boiled down good, she would add rice and black pepper and continue to cook it until the rice was done.

125

CARSON NAVAL STORES COMPANY
FACTORS AND WHOLESALE GROCERS

Savannah Ga. Dec. 18th. 1930

SPIRITS OF TURPENTINE

Turpentine has continued in fairly good demand, with only small fluctuations. Todays sales were 284 barrels at 35¾¢.

Receipts today	464	against	638	last year.
Receipts to date this month	9,393	"	7,819	"
Receipts since April 1st.	179,088	"	175,779	"
Savannah stock today	25,995	"	15,845	"
Jacksonville stock today	23,795	"	23,477	"
London stock today	58,126	"	36,397	"

R O S I N

The past few days the rosin market has advanced slightly. The demand is somewhat better.

Quotations today: FIRM	Quotations yesterday: FIRM	Quotations year ago: FIRM
X 7.15	X 7.15	X 8.55
W W "	W W "	W W 8.50
W G 6.45	W G 6.45	W G 8.00
N 5.10	N 5.10	N 7.60
M 4.55	M 4.55	M 7.25
K 4.20	K 4.20	K 7.20
I 4.07½	I 4.00	I "
H "	H "	H "
G 4.05	G "	G "
F 4.00	F 3.95	F "
E 3.95	E 3.90	E 7.10
D 3.75	D 3.70	D 7.05
B 3.55	B 3.55	B 7.00
Sales 275	Sales 562	Sales 1,158

Savannah stock today 192,019 against 141,541 on same day last year.
Jacksonville " 131,220 " 112,023 on same day last year.

chc

Yours very truly,

CARSON NAVAL STORES COMPANY

No.1,120

CHIPPING REPORT

NAME		AMOUNT CHIPPED	AT	AMOUNT	
Robert Hughes	Pull	8.900	90	8 01	✓
Babe Hall	"	6.700	"	✓ 89	✓
Alex Simons	"	1.000	"	90	✓
Will Mason	"	5.500	"	4 95	✓
Dan Hall	"	6.000	"	✓ 40	✓
Joe Lewis	"	2.500	"	2 25	✓
Alton Lewis Neg	"	7.000	1.10	7 70	✓
Curtis Lewis	"	5.400	1.10	✓ 94	✓
Henry Turner Team		5 Days		6 25	✓

CHIPPED OUT THIS WEEK?

WHAT CROPS NOT CHIPPED?

WHAT DRIFTS NEED DIPPING?

NUMBER STREAKS ON ABOVE?

REMARKS: | WOODSMAN | WEEK ENDING 10/16/37

FORM NO. 102 - COPYRIGHT PENDING. TURPENTINE DISTRIBUTING CO.

A woman asked her husband, "Why are you sharpening that razor?" "Woman, there's a pair of strange shoes under your bed. If there ain't no man in them shoes, I'm going to use this razor to shave."

For ground itch, take the root of bear grass and steep it in hot water to soften it. Then strain and mix the juice with turpentine to make it to a soft poultice. Bind the affected area.

6/5 6/12 6/19 6/26 —   1937

NAME	1ST WEEK	2ND WEEK	3RD WEEK	4TH WEEK	5TH WEEK	TOTAL	
Hao Williams	3 00						
Sam Hall	5 25						
Geo Jackson	4 00						
Bob Hall	7 25						
Robt Hughs	2 50						
Alton Lewis	4 60						
Jee Lewis	2 00						
John Small	3 25						
Tom Chapman	4 00						
Joe Walker	6 00						
James Bradham	1 25						
Geo Williams	5 00						
Joe Reese	3 50						
Gus Bope	3 60						
J W Washington	6 30						
H Dixon	1 50						
McKenas	2 25						
Jas Hare	3 70						
Jim Haro	3 00						
Justin Brown	2 50 / 1 10						
Elvira Carter	2 50						

FORM NO. 101 - COPYRIGHT PENDING. TURPENTINE DISTRIBUTING CO.

For heartburn and indigestion, chew a few
pine needles and swallow the juice.

What is the extreme penalty for bigamy?
Two mothers-in-law.

CARSON NAVAL STORES COMPANY
FACTORS AND WHOLESALE GROCERS

Savannah, Ga.
Feb. 13th 1930

In purchasing "DIP BARRELS" consider the material from which they are made. "DIPS" are manufactured from:

Prime spirit barrel stock

#2 White oak stock

Culled spirit barrel staves

#1 Red oak staves

#2 Red oak staves

The cheaper red oak staves are more porous and more liable to leakage than white oak staves. Barrels made therefrom can be sold at a considerably lower price.

#1 White Oak is the best material and is worth a reasonable difference in price. Do not buy "Dips" because of a cheap quotation; ascertain what you are to get and pay a little more, if necessary, to secure a serviceable barrel.

You can buy your dip barrels from us as advantageously as from any other source, get our prices before buying.

Yours very truly,

CARSON NAVAL STORES COMPANY

For fellons put pine tar on cotton and bind it onto the fellon to draw it out at one. Be ready to open in just a short time.

For a crick in the neck, wrap Spanish moss around it. The chiggers will soon make you forget the stiff neck. Rub turpentine on the chigger bites for relief.

CONSOLIDATED NAVAL STORES COMPANY

ACCOUNTING of LOAN from COMMODITY CREDIT CORPORATION on

165 Bbls. / _____ Drums } Gum Rosin, Marked _Wakulla_ Rec'd _Jan_, 19____

DATE	WAREHOUSE RECEIPT NUMBER			NO. BBLS.	GRADE	WEIGHT	PRICE	AMOUNT	
	X	thru	X		X		6.90		
	WW	"	WW		WW		6.90		
	WG	"	WG	5	WG	2570	6.60	59	40
	N	"	N	10	N	5055	6.40	115	54
	M	"	M	17	M	6015	6.20	113	19
	K	"	K	25	K	12480	6.00	267	43
	I	"	I	34	I	17035	5.85	3591	
	H	"	H	36	H	18070	5.75	371	08
	G	"	G	43	G	21685	5.60	433	70
	F	"	F		F		4.25		
	E	"	E		E		4.00		
	D	"	D		D		3.75		
	B	"	B		B		3.25		
		TOTAL		165		82860		1736	25
	LESS: Retain of 60c per bbl. or 75c per drum							99	00
						Gross Amount		$1637	25

CHARGES:

Freight	$140	25
Storage	11	55
Inspection. Cooperage and Weighing	9	90
Insurance	8	18
Commission 1¼ per cent.	8	18	178	06
Net Proceeds, Collected and Credited 6/14 1939	E. & O. E.	$1459	19

(884)

To Wakulla Turp Co
Wakulla
Fla

View of the turpentine still with the cooling tub and collector barrel in building to the left. In the foreground is the firebox and chimney. This type of still was first used in the industry in 1834 for distilling resin from the pine trees.

"Say," said the preacher, "I ain't saw you here at the meetin' house for a considerable time." "That's so," replied Bull Johnson, "I've been very busy." "Well, how come you're here tonight?" "Well, you see, it's like this preacher, I was repairing a chicken coop for some gentleman and I got a situation where I got to put a fence around a watermelon patch for another gentleman and I needs kind of special guidance from temptation."

For skin rash and itch, take hog lard and rich tar from fat lighter wood. Heat it and allow it to cool. Then apply it to the itch.

I asked Mary, "How can you tell an old chicken from a young one?" Mary said, "By the teeth, ma'am." "How silly - a chicken has no teeth." "No, but I have."

131

Chit'lins

Sections of the small intestines are put in a jar of salt water and allowed to sit for three or four days. Then they are taken out, rinsed, washed and rinsed again. In winter they can be lightly salted, put in the jars and kept for a few days before cooking. When cooking, cut up into small pieces and remove any unwanted layers of lining, then boil in salt water with pepper until it is tender. Dip in a batter of flour, water and egg. Or, roll in cornmeal and fry in hog lard. We stripped our chit'lins (cleaned them) in the River when possible. The clean running water washed all of the "stuff" down stream. When we weren't near the river we would clean them in a hole dug in the yard which was later filled in. Once we were sitting at the table eating chit'lins that mama had fixed along with greens and bread. The chit'lins were fried. One of the boys from a nearby city who was working in the woods with us, was eating with us. He was a little touchy about eating chit'lins so I took a few grains of corn and put it in my pocket. After we got to eating our plate of chit'lins, greens and cornbread I pulled a grain of corn out of my pocket and flipped in up on my plate and said, "Look what I got out of my chit'lins, somebody didn't clean these very well." That ended the city boys eating of our chit'lins.

A new preacher by the name of Ham came into the camp. One of the old women didn't understand his name when he was introduced. After the sermon was over, she rushed down to him and said, "What is your name?" "Sister," he replied, "my name is the best part of the hog." "I sure is glad to meet you Mr. Chitterlings"

As you can see, no part of the animal was wasted. We usually ate the whole hog, except the squeal. We also cooked cows' tripe, which was the stomach of the cow. It was boiled much like the chit'lins of the hog. After boiling it was cut into squares, floured and fried in hog lard. Wild game was usually cooked in the same manner, with small game being floured and fried like chicken if they were young. If they were old they were cooked as squirrel and rice, or squirrel and dumplings. Almost all of the wild animals that we killed would be used in some way, even if we had to take it home and cook it for the dogs. We had a limited number of bullets for the rifle or shells for the shotgun because of the Depression and the Second World War. We knew that if we went hunting with five shells, we had better bring back five pieces of meat to show for them. There was no target practicing or just shooting away bullets.

Liniment. Mix an equal amount of gum camphor and turpentine and rub it on.

An old hand was killed in an accident. After he died the insurance adjuster went to investigate. "Did Washington P. Johnson live here?" he asked the weeping woman who opened the door. "Yes sir." she replied between sobs. "I want to see the remains." With a new sense of importance, the dusty widow drew herself erect and answered proudly, "I am the remains."

132

Chicken

We always had to prepare our own chicken all the way from the barnyard to the table for cooking, . We would build a fire under the wash pot and heat clean water, take the chicken that we wanted to kill, pick him up by the head, wring his neck, throw him down and let him flop until he was dead, then scald him in the hot water, and pick the feathers off. Most of the feathers were used for either bed or pillow filling. After all the feathers were off the chicken still had little hairs on it so we would take a piece of old newspaper or catalog pages (yes, we used catalog pages for other things, too) and set it on fire. As it blazed up the chicken would be passed through it, holding it by the legs and neck. This action singed the hair off the skin. Then we would take out the entrails, saving the liver, gizzards and other things that were edible which would be cleaned and cooked, too. From this point we would cook it according to what it was. If it was a fryer, a young chicken, we would fry it in the typical way of frying chicken. If it was an older chicken or an old rooster it might be cooked in dumplings or purlow, using the same simple recipes to cook it. Other fowls of the farm, turkeys, geese, ducks were basically prepared the same way, whether tame or wild.

Dough Boys with Fish

Take the meal mixture that you breaded the fish in and add an egg to it. Mix it with milk and stir it up. Spoon it one spoonful at a time into the hot fish grease and fry it until it is golden brown. The batter will slip off the spoon better if the spoon is wet.

The turpentine hand was riding his mule along the road. The Man came by in his big automobile and stopped to ask the old turpentine hand if he wanted a ride. He said, "Yes sir, I'd like to ride." He said, "Well, what are you going to do with your mule?" He said, "I'll just let him follow along behind." "Well, do you think he can stay with us?" "Oh, yessir, he can stay with us." So they got in the car and started on down the road with the old mule running along behind them. The Man stepped up to about 30 mph and the old mule still ran right along behind. He stepped up to about 45 and the old mule was still there. He went up to 55 mph and the old mule was still right behind them. The Man turned to the turpentine hand and said "Man, that mule can really run." The hand said, "Yessir, he's a pretty good runner." So they stepped up to about 65 and The Man looked in the rear view mirror and said, "That mule's got his tongue hanging out now." " Which side of his mouth is it hanging out of, Boss?" " It's hanging out of the left side." "Well, get a little further over to the right, he's signaling to pass."

"Was your uncle's life insured?" "No, when he died, he was a total loss."

For headaches, sleep on a pillow filled with pine needles.

For consumption, chew the inner bark of a white pine.

For lung congestion, pour boiling water over turpentine and inhale the steam off it.

GLOSSARY

Apron- A metal strip inserted into a tree just above the cup to direct the flow of gum into the cup.

AT FA - American Turpentine Farmers Association. Supposedly organized in 1936 in Valdosta, GA, however the author thinks this was a reorganization because there is correspondence from the organization dating back to before the Depression.

Bar - The unworked portion of the tree, between faces on a two or three faced tree.

Batting Dross - Remains from the straining of the rosin in the bottom strainer.

Box (Cup) - Cavity or container used to catch the gum at the base of the tree or at the beginning streak of the year.

Box Hoe - Tool for cleaning (raking) grass and straw away from trees so fire wouldn't burn the face

Box Stump - Tree stump with box cut into it that collected gum.

Boxing Trees - The act of cutting holes in the bases of trees or placing cups on trees for collecting gum.

Breast High - Four and a half feet high. The point on a tree where diameter measurements are taken. D.B.H.

Bung - Filler hole in barrel

Canopy - The leafy crown of trees.

Cap'm - What the hands called The Man when they were speaking directly to him.

Car-boy - A bottle or rectangular container of about 5 to 15 gallon capacity for liquids. Often cushioned in a special container.

Cat Face - Scars left on trees after chipping or burning.

CCC - Commodities Credit Corporation.

Charge - Kettle full of raw gum.

Charging - Emptying the gum barrels into the copper still kettle

Chipping Boxes - The act of making streaks (scars) on trees.

Commissary - Supply store at the camp.

Commissary Coins - Coins (money) that the hands were paid in which could only be used at the company commissary.

Commissary Weddin' - Marriage of a couple in camp.

Condenser - Water filled container that held the condensing coils.

Condensing Coils - Copper coils that the water and turpentine vapor (steam) pass through while cooling to liquid form for placing into the first separating barrel.

Cooper - Barrel maker

Cooperage - Wood from which barrels and kegs are made.

Cote-house Weddin - Marriage of a couple at the county seat by the county judge with "a pair o'" licenses.

Cotton Batting - Cotton used in bottom rosin strainer.

Crop - 10,000 faces - 10 drifts.

Croze - Cooper's tool.

Cup - See box.

D.B.H. - See breast high.

Dehydrator - Barrel used in the final act of separating water from distilled turpentine.

Dip - See Gum.

Dip Bucket - Same as gum bucket.

Dip Iron - Tool for removing gum deposits from box or cup.

Dipping - The act of removing the gum from the cup.

Dips - Dip barrels.

Distiller (Stiller) - Operator of the still.

Dock - Platforms for storing barrels of gum, turpentine, or rosin.

Drift - 1,000 faces.

Dross - Residue strained from rosin after cooking is completed.

Face (Cat Face) - Scars left on a tree from turpentine operation.

Factors - Brokers

Fire Box - Area below and around the kettle for firing (heating) the charge.

Fire Lane or Break - A strip in the forest kept clear of flammable material as protection against the spread of fire.

Gear - See Turpentine Wagon.

Gum - Liquid that bled from the trees after the streaks on the trees were made. Also called crude gum.

Gum Barrel - Container for transporting gum from the woods to the still.

Gum Bucket - Container for collecting gum for transportation to the gum barrel.

Gum Line - The level to which the still kettle was filled with a charge.

Gutter - A V shaped metal strip installed above the cup to direct the flow of gum into the container.

Hack - Cutting tool for making "streaks" on trees up to about breast height.

Hand - Man that worked in the turpentine woods or helper at the still.

Head - Top of barrel.

High Pulled Gum - Resin from trees where the faces are 8 to 10 feet high (last years of working.)

Hoop - Metal ring for holding barrel staves together.

Hoop Iron - Thin flat metal strips for making barrel hoops. Widths vary from 1" to 2".

Kettle (Copper still kettle) - Used for cooking the gum.

Light Wood - Heart pine wood left after sap wood rots off the tree.

Low Wine - Water in the separator barrel.

Naval Stores - A term applied to turpentine and rosin. This term comes from the early use of turpentine products in shipbuilding.

Oil of Turpentine - See spirits of turpentine.

Operator - A producer of Naval Stores.

Pitch - The resin of a coniferous tree or a thick tar made from it.

Pull - Cutting tool for making "streaks" on trees from breast height to the top of the face.

Quarters - Area in the camp where the hands lived.

Quarters House - Where the hands lived.

Raised Cup Gum - Resin from trees where the cups have been moved up to the level of new working of the face.

Raking Boxes - The act of removing grass and straw from around the base of trees to protect them from fire.

Ramp - Used for rolling barrels up to different levels or docks at the still.

Red Cockaded Woodpecker - Endangered species. Zebra backed with a black cap. The white cheek is an obvious field mark. The tiny red cockade of the male is hard to see. Habitat: Open piney woods.

Resin - See Gum.

Rock Salt - Ice cream salt. Salt used in the dehydration to separate the remaining water from the turpentine.

Rosin - Remains in the bottom of the still after cooking.

Rosin Barrel - Barrel used for transporting rosin from the still to the market.

Rosin Clarification - The process of straining rosin to remove impurities. Usually three levels: wire, screen and cotton.

Rosin Vat - The vat that the pure rosin was collected in from which it was moved after cooking and straining.

Round - Bottom of barrel.

Sap wood - The outer part of a tree, composed of living cells.

Scrape - Gum that collects on face during the chipping "streaking" operation (March - October.)

Scrape Bucket - Container for collecting scrape from trees for transport to the gum barrel.

Scrape Iron - Tool for removing gum deposits from "face."

Scrub - See shrub.

Separator Barrel - Barrel used for separating the distilled turpentine from the water.

Shrub - A woody plant not attaining tree size or form.

Side Camp - Living quarters for hands away from the main camp. See Turpentine Camp.

Slash - 1) Waste from a logging operation. 2) A species of pine.

Spirits - See Turpentine.

Spirits of Turpentine - The primary product of the distillation process.

Staves - Boards for building barrels.

Still - Distillery for cooking the gum into turpentine and rosin.

Streaks - Cuts (scars) made into trees by chipping.

Stumpage - Standing timber.

Sulfate Pulping - Creation of turpentine by the condensation of vapors which produce sulfate turpentine and tall oil.

Sulfate Turpentine - Product of sulfate pulping.

Sulfuric Acid - Used to increase the flow of gum from the slash pine.

Tail Gate - Drain in bottom of still where rosin is released after a charge is cooked.

Tall Oil - Product of sulfate pulping.

Tally Man - Person who kept count of the number of trees boxed or chipped by each hand.

Tallywhacker - A stick or club carried by the tally man, used to hit a tree and make a whacking noise to let a hand know that his job was not properly done.

The Man - Supervisor of the turpentine operation.

Timber - Standing trees.

Tins - Gutters and aprons nailed to face to direct gum into the cup.

Tram - Railroad car used to transport logs and turpentine out of the woods.

Tram Road - Road used to transport logs and turpentine out of the woods.

Tub - See Condenser.

Tunk - A house where the hands and women in camp gathered to dance, drink 'shine, gamble and fight.

Turpentine - Clear liquid rendered from steam from gum while cooking.

Turpentine Barrel (Spirit Barrel) - Barrel used for transporting distilled turpentine from the still to the market.

Turpentine Camp - Living area, usually deep in the woods, where The Man, Distiller, Woods Rider and Hands lived. It usually had a still, commissary, and other facilities to make it self supporting.

Turpentine Shanty - Lean-to type shed in the turpentine woods where the hands could get out of the inclement weather.

Turpentine Wagon (Dip Wagon) - Wagon for transporting barrels from the woods to the still.

Turpentining - The process of working trees to obtain resin or gum. May also include the distilling process.

Vat - See Rosin Vat.

Virgin Forest - A forest which has not been cut over. Old growth.

Virgin Gum - Resin from trees in the first year of working.

Virgin Cup or Box - First cup or box placed on a tree.

Whet Stone - Hone for sharpening hacks, pulls, and scrape irons.

Wood Naval Stores - Creation of turpentine from stumps, knots and hearts of pines.

Woods Rider - Supervisor of the hands working the trees.

Worm - Copper cooling coil in the condenser. Condensing coils.

Yearling Gum - Resin from trees in the second year of working.

VALUE GUIDE

NVA - No value available

The values listed in this guide are the average of asking prices for comparable items sold at auctions, in antique stores and by collectors in the Southeastern United States. If I saw a price listed or item sold that was, in my opinion, out of line I didn't use it. I will not attempt to price items that are commonly found in antique books, such as unexcavated name brand tools or cast iron cookware. I have never found or excavated Griswold cast iron or Stanley tools around camp sites, cooper shops, blacksmith shops or turpentine stills.

I am unable to list a value on many items simply because the items are no longer available. Over the past twenty years naval stores industry related artifacts have been bought up by collectors and have almost totally disappeared from the market.

The values shown in this book should be used only as a guide. Prices vary greatly and are affected by demand as well as individual item condition. Neither the author nor the publisher assumes responsibility for losses that may be incurred as a result of consulting this guide.

Page	Item	
6	Turpentine in bottle/label	$ 15
6	Pine tar soap	4
10	ATFA Calendar	30
27	Box stump	NVA
35	Cup cover	NVA
36	Lightwood knot (virgin pine)	NVA
36	Cups	
	a. Herty cup	10
	b. Pringle (oblong clay)	16
	c. Birdseye (galvanized metal)	18
	d. Buzzard wing (galvanized metal)	24
	e. Buzzard wing (aluminum)	18
	f. Oblong (latest type - galvanized metal)	5
	Oblong (latest type - aluminum)	5
	g. Experimental (very rare)	NVA
	Aprons and gutters (galvanized metal or aluminum)	3/pr
47	Axes	
	a. Box with handle	100+
	b. Broad	85+
	c. Box without handle	70+
47	Wood maul	35-65

Page	Item	
Page	**Item**	
48	Dip Irons	
	a. Box (hand forged - very rare)	NVA
	b. Box (hand forged - rare)	$65
	c. Herty cup (hand forged - very rare)	NVA
	d. Metal cup (factory made)	18
49	Scrape Irons	
	Push down (hand forged - very rare)	NVA
	Push down (factory made)	20
49	Hacks and Hogals	
	With handle, rings and weight ball	90
	Without handle (bill only)	20
50	Pull	
	With handle	70
	Without handle (bill only)	20
51	Scrape Irons	
	Pull down with handle	80
	Pull down without handle	30
52	Cup cover	NVA
53	Scrape bucket	125
54	Dip bucket	125
54	Yo-yo with handle (very rare)	NVA
54	Yo-yo without handle (rare)	NVA
55	Dip wagon	NVA
56	Hoe (for raking boxes)	30
56	Hoe (top left - for kitchen use)	60
57	Tin puller	80+
57	Whetstone (round for sharpening bills)	NVA
58	Snake's head railroad rail (very rare)	NVA
58	Railroad rail 2 1/2" (logging tram)	NVA
58	Railroad spike (for snake's head rail)	NVA
58	Railroad spike 4" (for 2 1/2" rail)	8
63	Tree planter	450
63	Circular saw/wheels (operable)	600
64	Hornet's nest 12" x 18"	35
81	Stove (Quarter's house)	350
85	Marble (home made)	NVA
85	Button (oyster shell)	8
85	Button (bone)	3
85	Dice (bone)	NVA
86	Seal (1860)	45
86	Comb (bone)	NVA
90	Corn sheller	70
90	Cane stripper	28

The Illustrated History of the Naval Stores (Turpentine) Industry

The Illustrated History of the Naval Stores Industry is a culmination of many years of enjoyable research by the author. Pete Gerrell has portrayed the history of the turpentine industry through the use of old photos, letters, advertisements, home remedies, recipes and jokes. This 148 page illustrated history traces the industry from Biblical times through the years to it's virtual finish in the 1970's.

Copyright TXU 814-159   1997 by Pete Gerrell

ISBN 0-9665193-0-2

Library of Congress Catalog Card No. 98-90418

To order copies complete the information below and send order blank with check or money order to: SYP Publishing c/o Pete Gerrell
P.O. Box 627   Crawfordville, FL 32326

NAME: _____

Address: _____

City, State, Zip: _____

Send _____ copies of "The Illustrated History of the Naval Stores Industry" @ $19.95 each $_____

Postage & Handling @ $3.00 per book $_____

Florida Residents add 7% tax $_____

Total amount enclosed $_____

VIDEOCONFERENCING SKILLS

Career Solutions Training Group
Paoli, PA

Writer:
John J. Champa, Ph.D.
Director
Multimedia Services & Consulting
UNISYS

THOMSON

SOUTH-WESTERN

Australia · Canada · Mexico · Singapore · Spain · United Kingdom · United States

SOUTH-WESTERN

THOMSON LEARNING

10-Hour Series: Videoconferencing Skills

By Career Solutions Training Group

Editor-in-Chief
Jack Calhoun

Vice President/Executive Publisher
Dave Shaut

Team Leader
Karen Schmohe

Acquisitions Editor
Joseph Vocca

Project Manager
Laurie Wendell

Production Manager
Tricia Matthews Boies

Production Editor
Alan Biondi

Director of Marketing
Carol Volz

Marketing Manager
Chris McNamee

Marketing Coordinator
Lori Pegg

Design Project Manager
Stacy Jenkins Shirley

Cover and Internal Design
Joe Pagliaro Design

Manufacturing Coordinator
Charlene Taylor

Compositor
settingPace LLC

Printer
Edwards Brothers, Inc.
Ann Arbor, MI

Preface

Welcome to Videoconferencing Skills

There is no other book like this in the world. It was not written by a marketing department, or with the purpose of selling videoconferencing equipment. This book is based on the solid, real-life, field-tested experiences of mature business and academic people who have used videoconferencing technology over the years to accomplish their goals.

Skills in videoconferencing, fundamentally, are good meeting management skills, with the addition of special videoconferencing equipment to be used and a few unique protocols to follow. Similarly, the skills acquired in running an effective videoconference carry over well to all other kinds of electronic collaboration or e-meetings, such as audioconferencing and webconferencing.

Collectively, these various types of interrelated e-meeting skills are increasingly essential tools in the modern business and academic environments. At many points in your career, you will be required to demonstrate teamwork and leadership, even if it is only to ensure that your assignment requiring the assistance of others gets accomplished. One of the best ways to demonstrate leadership is to call for a meeting. But, if the working group is spread over a large geographic area, physically bringing people together can be difficult and expensive. A videoconference is the answer.

During the weeks following the tragedies of September 11, 2001, a study by the National Business Travel Association showed that 88 percent of the companies surveyed planned to increase their use of videoconferencing. In addition to facing concerns about their employees' safety, many companies are now considering the technology as a way to save money in a shrinking economy and avoid the time constraints now imposed by greater airport security. Videoconferencing and online collaboration are viable, cost-effective alternatives.

Features

Videoconferencing Skills offers students and instructors a book that begins with basic information and moves to concepts that are more complex. The topics are interesting and challenging, focusing on the tools needed to present dynamic and forceful videoconference meetings. Using a fast-paced, interesting format, this book provides just the right amount of detail to help a beginner start developing videoconferencing skills.

The ten lessons in *Videoconferencing Skills* provide:

- An activity-driven approach with three to five activities in each lesson
- Relevant and instructional illustrations
- An introduction to the equipment used in videoconferencing
- Suggestions for making every conference successful
- Instructions in preparing PowerPoint® slides for a videoconference

- Internet activities that expand the discussion of videoconferencing

- Team activities that can be completed in pairs or groups

- A glossary of terms that should be part of every videoconference user's vocabulary

The *Videoconferencing Skills Instructor's Manual* provides a wide array of support materials, teaching suggestions, team activities, and Internet activities. Additionally, tests, guidelines for evaluation, and complete solutions are also provided.

About the Author

For 17 years, John Champa has worked as a systems integration engineer, outsourcing contact, infrastructure specialist, server technologist, and consultant to Unisys in the areas of videoconferencing, wireless local area networks (WLAN), and related technologies. He has written many white papers and articles on the topic of videoconferencing and has filed four U.S. patent applications in the area. He is listed in Marquis' *Who's Who in Science and Engineering*.

In addition to being certified as a telecommunications engineer by the National Association of Radio and Telecommunications Engineers (NARTE) since 1986, he has been an active FCC licensed amateur radio operator or "Ham" (callsign K8OCL) since 1959 and did early work in Amateur Television (ATV) two-way communications. John is also chairman of the American Radio Relay League (the national association of radio amateurs) for the High-Speed Digital and Multimedia Working Group. His appointment was, in part, recognition of his pioneering work in the area of amateur digital video communications. When not playing with wireless and other hi-tech toys, John loves to hunt, fish, hike, camp, and canoe the beautiful outdoors in remote areas of North America and Africa.

Author's Acknowledgments

It is impossible to thank the hundreds of business executives, project managers, and engineers who have shared their videoconference experiences with me since August, 1988, when I set up the first two Unisys videoconference rooms—in what was then Burroughs Worldwide Headquarters (Detroit, MI) and Sperry Corporate Headquarters (Blue Bell, PA). Now both sites are part of Unisys. I am grateful for their assistance and have attempted to incorporate as much of that helpful information as possible in this text.

However, I must acknowledge the specific assistance of my professional videoconferencing colleagues in the preparation of this textbook: Dave Frymier, Lee Chapin, and Jim Dougherty of Unisys Information Technology management for their leadership and support; Patrick Carr, Rosalie Coey, Jim Miller of Unisys Videoconferencing Network Operations for their encouragement and suggested improvements; Rhonda Raymond of Unisys Information Technology for her helpful suggestions on videoconference slide preparation; Bill Patton of Unisys Video

Implementation Engineering for his always-insightful observations; Henry Grove, a videoconference consultant of international acclaim, for being my mentor and adviser on many complicated issues over the years; George Wilson, videoconference engineer, who taught me the valuable contributions that TV broadcasting technology made to this branch of telecommunications; Jamie Poindexter, University of Wisconsin-Extension; and Fred Knight, editor and publisher of *Business Communications Review* who helps me keep up with the latest and greatest in video telecommunications technology. But most of all, I must express my deepest appreciation and warmest possible regards to my best friend and companion, Karen Lynn Feder, art teacher extraordinaire, for putting up with my long hours at the laptop needed to get all the valuable collective ideas and revelations into this book.

Reviewers

The author and publisher wish to acknowledge the following educators, trainers, and consultants who provided valuable feedback during the development of *Videoconferencing Skills:*

Daphne Zito
Department Chairperson
Business, Medical, Legal Office Administration
Katharine Gibbs School
Melville, NY

Nichol W. Free
Computer Instructor
Computer Learning Network
Mechanicsburg, PA

Mary M. Davey
Instructor, Desktop Applications Specialist
Computer Learning Network
Mechanicsburg, PA

Shirley Solano
MOUS Training & Certification Director
Westchester Business Institute
White Plains, NY

Contents

What Is Videoconferencing?

Focus

"Visual images can have a greater and more lasting impact than words alone."

—Julian Goldstein & Jeremy Goldstein in
Videoconferencing Secrets

Communicating by Video

Videoconferencing is the use of digital video and audio technology for two-way communication across long distances. Most often, organizations use videoconferences to reach a large number of people in separate locations. A videoconference is less time-consuming and much less expensive than the travel costs of bringing together the same number of participants in one location for a presentation.

Thousands of businesses and services throughout the U.S. use videoconferencing technology daily. They train their staffs in distant cities, hold sales meetings, review the status of projects, troubleshoot production problems, monitor security, and even diagnose illnesses.

Figure 1-1: Communicating by video

In the Beginning

Videoconferencing traces its origins to the mid-1960s when AT&T demonstrated its *Picture Phone* at the 1964 New York World's Fair. About the same time, the cartoon TV series *The Jetsons* showed a futuristic family using TV for two-way communications with friends and family.

Just because something is possible is not enough to make it popular for every day activities. It must also be affordable and practical. For videoconferencing, these conditions were not reached until almost two decades after its introduction.

Progress

In the mid-1980s manufacturers started to produce videoconferencing systems on a large scale, which brought prices down to a level that commercial users could afford. Telephone companies developed special lines, called **digital circuits,** to send television programs and two-way video signals around the country, making it possible for large

9. one-way audio and video viewed over the Internet

10. videoconference facilities and equipment available for rent from phone companies and public libraries

```
V B X R N B N H L K N L W L T V X Z Y N Z L X H B W Y Q
O Y Q W M B N R K R C G M T Y N F S H C H B L K L Z M N
I B K R Q T X D C B P T M R D T T B J G H Z L L P N O T
C M C B M H D M I L R J R N M I R B N N M D Z L Y K O L
E U D H T T D C Q G K W W W U Y R Y F J N F W P K W R L
S L K W M C T K X Z I X T C M N K T R C C P V H N H E B
W T X R D T H K G K X T R H R M G R H M P Y W L B X C T
I I M B Y Y K L M V L I A R R F B A R X G K V F K W N G
T P N W Y R H Y L R C B Q L H F I K V J P F R P N Z E N
C O V R F J B T N L V V T T N R B K Z P N M L J Y P R I
H I N D B F M J A G L K R Z M E Y T W M T N T R D G E C
E N T F V L X T N Q F T C A Z C T L S N Y R Z L J K F N
D T T T Z R I C R V K M N N N L W W M A D V V G L T N E
V V C G P G L R R W V C W W X N J L O K C D Y H Y M O R
I I L H I Z T X M Z O N X X D W L D J R P B F Z R J C E
D D K D N Y W K X N G B Z V V P P M C K T E J Y K O F
E E G Y F L K T T T M K N R Z C Q L T X P D M W L L E N
O O Z Q G K X R K J V H D B C Q N J T K X G P L Z T D O
C C T X R Y O T F Q J F C L C B K L V N X Y R C T B I C
O O R R M L M M E C N E S E R P S U O U N I T N O C V O
N N L M L C K K C J R K V W R T Z L H N W K Q N J R C E
F F W E V H F L H L T N V Z N H G K T D K P R R Q P I D
E E D N K N H N M L V D F H J F Z L N M B T B W D J L I
R R T Y G M Q N T N T X Q T W N H L D G W M M M J P B V
E E D C O M P R E S S I O N A L G O R I T H M S D F U Q
N N V H T D W G B K N Y G C N T R V N Y H N K G B M P N
C C J R R W Q K M L H B B L F M T P Q V P L L K M H F T
E E P R N B N M G M Y K T T D Y W R V Z N Q T P K F Z N
```

© South-Western, a division of Thomson Learning. Made using 1-2-3 Word Search Maker™

Activity 1-2: Using Videoconferences

Organizations that might wish to use a videoconference to reach participants in different locations are listed below. In the blanks, write two purposes for which each organization might choose a videoconference for communicating.

AT&T   *Announce a reorganization*

                                  Describe a profit-sharing plan

American Red Cross

U.S. Department of State

American Medical Association

Sprint PCS

Michigan State University

Unisys

Public High School District

Chain of Business Schools

What is Videoconferencing?

Activity 1-3: Recommending Videoconference Type

Read the three case studies below and list the type of videoconference you would recommend in each situation. Choose a voice-switched conference, a chairman-controlled conference, or a continuous presence conference. Write the reasons for your recommendation.

Case Study 1

You are a technology manager for a restaurant chain with 300 locations across the country. The new software system that is used to create customer food checks and receive money has developed serious problems. Two people from the management division in Dallas and three people from the engineering division in Missoula, Montana, need to meet in a videoconference for one full day to decide how to handle the situation.

Type of videoconference recommended: _____

_____

Reasons for recommendation: _____

_____

_____

_____

_____

Case Study 2

The New York City life insurance company where you work wants to introduce a new investment plan that will be made available to its employees aged 25–55 who work in Atlanta, San Diego, Chicago, and Phoenix. The vice president of human resources asks you to arrange a presentation that will be received via a videoconference at each site.

Type of videoconference recommended: _____

_____

Reasons for recommendation: _____

_____

_____

_____

_____

Case Study 3

The athletic shoe company where you serve as a technical assistant in the videoconference center is developing a new lightweight shoe. Project teams from around the country need to meet to discuss their progress on various aspects of the shoe's development.

Type of videoconference recommended: _____

_____

Reasons for recommendation: _____

_____

_____

_____

_____

What is Videoconferencing?

Activity 1-4: Recommending Alternative Methods

Assume the company where you work does not have a videoconference center. Read the three case studies below and decide which alternative to attending a videoconference would be the most valuable in each situation. Choose VCR viewing at a later time, telephone hook-up to a videoconference, or public videoconference room. List the alternative method you recommend and the reasons for your recommendation.

Case Study 1

The vice president of a frozen food processing plant has not had an opportunity to visit offices in Omaha, Boston, Kansas City, and Seattle in the last year. Nevertheless, she would like new people in the offices to get to know her better and view her style of communication, even though she is unable to visit all the offices in person.

Recommendation: _____

_____

Reasons for recommendation: _____

_____

_____

_____

_____

_____

Case Study 2

The manager of engineering at an office furniture manufacturing company has questions regarding the design of the firm's new ergonomic chairs. He is unable to attend in person the videoconference that has been scheduled for discussion of the design problems. You arranged the videoconference, so he asks you to recommend how he can be involved in the conference.

Recommendation: _____

_____

Reasons for recommendation: _____

_____

_____

_____

_____

_____

Case Study 3

The new president of a regional bank headquartered in Chicago wants to meet by video-conference with all employees in the Milwaukee branch, but the branch does not have a videoconference room.

Recommendation: _____

_____

Reasons for recommendation: _____

_____

_____

_____

_____

_____

2 The Technical Points

Focus

"It's not the technology—not any more at least—but the videoconferencing skills that make the best meetings!"

—Henry Grove III
International Videoconferencing Consultant

Visual and Audio Quality of Videoconferences

Television video is designed for entertainment, so it requires sharp detail and superb color. When you watch TV shows, you can see small patterns in an actor's clothes, blood on the doctor's hands in an emergency room sequence, and antenna on a bug's head in a nature show. For two-way videoconferencing, less detail is needed.

Figure 2-1: Television quality is not necessary in a videoconference.

In a videoconference, the faces and facial expressions will be clear, and all images will be adequate for participants in other locations to see. However, the quality will not be as good as what you're used to viewing on television. Television broadcast images are transmitted using **analog** signals, electronic signals of varying frequency and amplitude. Videoconference software compresses these complex analog images into a series of simpler **digital** images with less detail. Digital images are transmitted simply as a string of 0s and 1s that can be read by a computer. This conversion from analog to digital signals is known as **digitalization,** or **coding.** It is performed by a computer called a COder-DECoder, **CODEC** for short.

Videoconferences run over the same long distance telephone lines as telephone calls and other electronic communications. Since a typical videoconference lasts about two hours, long distance telephone charges can add up quickly. By converting the analog signals to digital, and then compressing the information, the amount of information to be transmitted is greatly reduced along with the long distance charges. This can amount to substantial savings for a business.

The same type of digitalization and compression applies to the analog sound for videoconferences. In television or radio studios, the audio is handled very carefully so that the listener hears high fidelity and stereo sounds. Videoconferencing demands for audio are far less, and sound quality is considered adequate if participants can hear the voices clearly. The voices should sound natural, as if the speakers are really in the room with the listener. This is known as **presence,** or the perception that the person talking is actually present.

Making Connections

Connecting people in a variety of locations or cities to a human presenter in a central location or meeting place is the key concern during a videoconference. The most common method of connection is a **network design** or **network architecture,** which is a digital system of connected phone lines and computers. However, some videoconferences are sent over the same data communications networks used for e-mails and other electronic communications.

Telephone Digital Networks

A telephone digital network converts the human voice or other information into digital signals that can be sent over wire or fiber optic lines to their destination. The type used most often for video-conferences is the **Integrated Services Digital Network,** or **ISDN.** ISDN is a phone company standard for digital transmission over ordinary telephone copper wire as well as over other media. It allows for the fast transmission of large amounts of data and images. With an ISDN, you will dial up the location that is to receive the videoconference, just as you dial a voice-only telephone call.

© Artville/Getty Images, Inc.

Figure 2-2: **Network architecture connects phone lines and computers around the world.**

Usually, the dialing is handled through the automatic dialing function built into the CODEC. By entering the name of the receiving locations or individuals and their telephone numbers into the CODEC memory, you can use a remote control device to bring up the appropriate menu, then you can click at any time on the name of each location. The CODEC does the rest, and soon the remote location site appears on your TV screen. This system is called **videoconferencing switched network** or **H.320,** which is the name for the standard of quality for transmitting videoconference audio and video used by the **International Telecommunications Union (ITU).** The ITU, located in Geneva, Switzerland, is a United Nations organization that fosters cooperative international standards for telecommunications equipment and systems.

Video over the Internet

Until recently, most data networks such as the Internet were not designed to handle videoconferences because of network congestion with e-mails and other data. However, interest has grown for using the same networks for both data and video. With the advent of multimedia functions, such as web casting, data networks have become more robust and better able to handle videoconferences. Because of the increased capabilities of the Internet, you will see more Internet-based videoconference networks in the future. These networks are known as **Video over the Internet Protocol (VoIP).** They are known as **H.323** networks by data communications professionals, after the ITU standard for transmitting videoconferences over the Internet.

Gateways

At the present time network architecture for videoconferences are often **hybrid** networks; that is, they use both ISDN and VoIP networks. The two types of networks are connected by an electronic device called a **gateway** that allows them to operate as one network.

Multipoint Control Unit (MCU)

Most videoconferences involve three or more locations. Videoconferences showing in several locations are called multipoint videoconferences. A complex electronic system called a **videoconference bridge,** or **multipoint control unit (MCU)** is needed to connect multiple locations and conduct a multipoint videoconference. The videoconference **network coordinator** is the individual responsible for operating the bridge or MCU. This person calls the technician at each videoconference location and gives instructions on how to use the CODEC to connect to the bridge.

The type of multipoint videoconference (voice-switched, chairman-controlled, or continuous presence) will depend on the capabilities of the videoconference bridge. If the videoconference is not a multipoint videoconference but only a **point-to-point** call between two locations, the coordinator instructs the technician at each site to access the directory stored in the CODEC, and then to dial the desired location.

International Standards

The development of international standards for videoconferencing systems allows different locations to connect and interact, regardless of the brand of equipment or country of origin. Standards have been developed for network architectures, video compression, and audio compression. However, different locations may have different equipment capabilities. The videoconference network coordinator will help the technician at each site sort through these issues.

When combining the newer video and audio compression systems with older systems, quality may be lost. To reduce the probability of

Tip

To avoid transmission problems and poor quality, always find out what systems will be used at all sites participating in a videoconference. Any necessary upgrades and connection issues should be worked out well in advance of the conference.

this occurring, always ask the videoconference network coordinator about the capabilities of the videoconference equipment at each participating location.

If the videoconference system at one or more locations has older compression standards, request that the equipment and/or software be upgraded at the location before the meeting starts. This will allow all equipment systems in the videoconference to operate at their best quality. This is particularly important for training classes that often require higher video resolution and better voice quality. The following table shows the types of standards in use by videoconferencing professionals, their characteristics, and the abbreviations or designations that are used to refer to them.

Videoconferencing Standards

Standard	Network Requirements & Characteristics	Designations
Network architectures	Videoconferencing Switched Network Switch telephone digital circuits (Dial up)	ISDN or ITU H.320
	Video over Internet Protocol (Data)	VoIP, IP, or ITU H.323
Video compression	Powerful, one or two circuits needed Lower long distance charges	ITU H.263+
	Older, three ISDN circuits needed	ITU H.261
Audio compression	New, good quality	ITU G.722
	Older, less voice quality	ITU G.711

Activity 2-1: Matching Videoconferencing Terms

Match the following terms to the appropriate definitions.

a. analog signals   e. gateway   i. ISDN   m. point-to-point

b. CODEC   f. H.320   j. ITU   n. presence

c. digital data   g. H.323   k. network coordinator   o. videoconference bridge

d. digitization   h. hybrid network   l. network architecture

_____ 1. complex electronic signals of varying frequency and amplitude that produce high quality audio and video

_____ 2. data transmitted as a string of 0s and 1s that can be read by a computer; produces lower quality audio and video signals that can be transmitted faster

_____ 3. the conversion from analog to digital signals, another name for coding

_____ 4. computer that converts analog signals to digital data

_____ 5. the perception or feeling that a person talking in a videoconference is actually present in the room

_____ 6. a digital system of connected phone lines and computers, another name for network design

_____ 7. a phone company standard for digital transmission over ordinary telephone copper wire as well as over other media

_____ 8. ITU designation for videoconferencing switched network

_____ 9. International Telecommunications Union, the international union that creates cooperative standards for telecommunications systems

_____ 10. ITU designation for Internet-based videoconference networks

_____ 11. a network that uses both VoIP and ISDN networks

_____ 12. an electronic device that connects VoIP and ISDN networks and allows them to operate as one network

_____ 13. a complex electronic system needed to connect multiple locations and conduct a multipoint videoconference, another name for multipoint control unit

_____ 14. the individual responsible for operating the videoconference bridge or MCU during a videoconference

_____ 15. a videoconference between only two locations

The Technical Points

Activity 2-2: Identifying Video Quality

Television requires analog images while videoconferences require only digital images. For each image below, write *"A"* for *analog* or *"D"* for *digital* to identify which level of quality is needed. Explain your choice in the blanks provided.

_____ 1. A session to train heart surgeons stationed in third-world countries

_____
_____
_____

_____ 2. A cooking class for the chefs employed by a restaurant chain

_____
_____
_____

_____ 3. A presentation on the discoveries at an ancient archeological site

_____
_____
_____

_____ 4. A meeting of the marketing managers for a large company with locations in five countries

_____
_____
_____

_____ 5. A safety demonstration featuring snow boarding equipment

_____
_____
_____

Activity 2-3: Analyzing Sound Quality

Television and radio require analog quality sound while videoconferences require presence. For each sound listed below, write *"A"* for *analog* or *"P"* for *presence* to identify which level of quality is needed. Explain your choice in the blanks provided.

_____ 1. A national bookstore chain sponsors an author reading from one of her books to audiences at 40 of its bookstores

_____ 2. A music producer plays a new CD for reviewers to critique

_____ 3. A cattle food company makes a presentation about its products at a national gathering for students enrolled in agriculture programs

_____ 4. The president of an automobile manufacturing company introduces a new car model to dealers around the country

The Technical Points

Activity 2-4: Planning Coordination

List several items that should be coordinated with the videoconference network coordinator during the planning of a videoconference. Describe why these items are important to conducting a successful meeting.

Items to be coordinated   **Reason coordination is needed**

1. _____   _____

    _____

2. _____   _____

    _____

3. _____   _____

    _____

4. _____   _____

    _____

5. _____   _____

    _____

6. _____   _____

    _____

7. _____   _____

    _____

8. _____   _____

    _____

Activity 2-5: Making Recommendations

Make recommendations to the network coordinator for each videoconference described below.

1. The director of finance complains that long distance telephone charges are too high and that the method of videoconferencing may be the problem.

   _____

   _____

   _____

2. Though the sound during a videoconference is adequate for most participants, a few participants complain that the conference sound is tinny, like an inexpensive radio.

   _____

   _____

   _____

3. Recently, the network coordinator has spent more personal time than she likes dialing up the various locations for a multipoint videoconference. She's looking for a better and faster way to connect.

   _____

   _____

   _____

4. The technician at a British company with offices in the United States, Belgium, and Russia is worried that the systems at his location will provide low quality during the company's upcoming international conference.

   _____

   _____

   _____

The Technical Points

Activity 2-6: Analyzing Standards

The main impact of network standards has been to allow the equipment from various world-wide manufacturers to connect or "talk with" one another. Why is knowing the different levels or ages of standards important?

_____

_____

_____

_____

_____

Activity 2-7: Making Decisions

Write in the blanks the network or designation decisions you would make if you were the network coordinator in each videoconference situation described.

1. You want to reduce long distance charges. _____

   _____

2. You are asked to provide excellent sound quality. _____

   _____

3. Dial-up service is becoming dated, and you would like a more innovative way to deliver videoconferences. _____

   _____

   _____

The Technical Points

3 Audience, Location, and Timing

Focus

"Videoconferencing is a way to hold meetings that otherwise might not happen. Or, if they did happen, they'd be harder to set up, cost more money, and take more of everyone's time than they should."

—PictureTel Corporation
First-Timer's Guide to Videoconferencing

Nature of the Audience

While videoconferences come in all shapes and sizes, the most common ones consist of three or four individuals who meet for about two hours at three or four different locations or sites. Who attends, the location, and the timing are critical factors in the planning of any videoconference meeting, no matter the size of the event.

Number of Participants and Viewers

The first thing to consider when planning a videoconference is the seating capacity of each room that will be used for viewing the meeting. Keep in mind that the typical videoconference room is not designed as a theater. Often, it is a work or meeting area, so seating may be limited to the number of people who can be seated around a large table. That may mean as few as four or as many as ten or more participants. Don't invite a larger group than can be accommodated in the room.

Figure 3-1: Participants in a videoconference

Even rooms that provide additional seating in a gallery, or contain space for added tiers of chairs behind the table, have their limits. The participants seated in the gallery may be too far away from the TV screens to see significant details, or furniture or other participants may block their view of the TV screens. They may have difficulty clearly hearing the discussion. Further, they may be too far away from the control panel, the remote control device, or other visual equipment to exercise any effective control. If a gallery is used, only observers should sit there.

If the majority of participants at a videoconference site wish to observe the meeting but not participate, the videoconference network coordinator can have the session sent via live **video streaming** (one-way video and audio over a data network) to their personal computers. In this case, the actual videoconference room can be reserved exclusively for use by the active meeting participants.

Location of Sites Viewing the Videoconference

Videoconference sites, though similar, are designed with the specific requirements of the location in mind. Each site that is invited to attend a videoconference must be individually evaluated to determine if it will handle the number of participants who should be involved from the location. The videoconference network coordinator can often provide this information, but if not, the videoconference site/facility coordinator should be contacted directly.

Make the contact well in advance of the meeting and inquire as to both the seating capacity and type of room. Ask for details, such as the size of the TV screens at each site, especially if visual aids will be used. Microsoft PowerPoint® is the most popular format for slide designs. Knowing the size of the TV that is being viewed at each site and its distance from the viewers should influence the design of the slides. Slides will be covered in more detail in Chapter 6.

If the conference site has not been used previously, request a test session from the videoconference network coordinator in order to actually view the site and its seating arrangement. This reduces the embarrassment that could occur after the meeting opens when participants at all sites can see that seating is inadequate at one or more of the sites!

Geography and Time Zones

A meeting of two hours appears to be about the longest time most participants can sit without a break. If more than two hours is needed for a presentation, schedule time for breaks. If more than four hours are needed for the meeting, consider substituting a series of short meetings for one long meeting. This arrangement provides the additional advantage of a time interval to gather feedback, both positive and negative, from the participants.

Scheduling a two-hour videoconference to occur during an eight-hour day may not seem overly challenging. However, videoconference participants may be spread out over a large part of the earth. This is frequently the main justification for having the meeting via videoconference in the first place! Travel from each of the sites to one location would be expensive, time consuming and difficult, perhaps even dangerous. How does this affect planning for the conference?

Time zone differences pose a significant problem for videoconference planners. If, for example, a videoconference session is planned for 10 A.M. in a New York City office building, Los Angeles participants would have to be seated at their site by 7 A.M., probably an

hour before the start of their normal work day. (New York City is in the Eastern U.S. time zone, and Los Angeles is in the Pacific U.S. time zone, which is three hours behind.) Even if Los Angeles participants are asked to come at 7 A.M., arrangements will have to be made to open the building early and test all videoconference equipment to make sure it's fully operational. At such an early hour in Los Angeles, a light breakfast and beverages might be needed for participants.

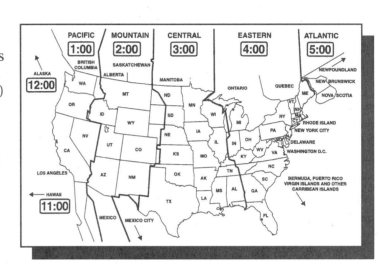

Figure 3-2: **North America Time Zones**

If a videoconference is scheduled for 10 A.M. Pacific Standard Time, participants at other locations would be scheduled as shown in the following table.

Time Zone Conversions

Pacific Standard Time	Mountain Standard Time	Central Standard Time	Eastern Standard Time	Atlantic Standard Time
10:00 A.M.	11:00 A.M.	12:00 P.M.	1:00 P.M.	2:00 P.M.

Meetings should be planned as far in advance as possible because videoconference rooms are heavily scheduled. The rooms may already be reserved by others, especially during the prime hours of 10 A.M. to 2 P.M. local time. By delaying the reservation of the room, the most advantageous time may be taken by another group.

Scheduling grows in complexity if participants from other continents such as Europe or Asia are invited. Those participants are operating in time zones that may be four or more hours later or earlier than the central site. At 10 A.M. in New York City, Europeans are nearing the end of their work day. For participants in Asia or the Pacific Rim countries, it is the middle of the night. Consult a time zone map or chart to be sure to schedule videoconferences at the most convenient time possible for all participants. Since there are 24 time zones, a worldwide videoconference will mean that some participants will be meeting during non-working hours. Consider the particular needs of such participants.

Tip

The Internet has many valuable resources for time zone conversion charts and maps. Visit one of the following sites for information that can help you determine appropriate times for meetings that cross time zones.

- The Astronomical Applications Department of the U.S. Naval Observatory—http://aa.usno.navy.mil

- Convert It.com—www.convertit.com

- Time Zone Converter—www.timezoneconverter.com

- Time and Date.com—www.timeanddate.com

Language and International Considerations

Videoconferencing has a unique advantage over other forms of electronic telecommunications because participants can see all the other participants! This is especially helpful when English is not the first language of some of the people attending the meeting or when cultural differences influence the communication style.

Much of human communication is nonverbal. Facial expressions, hand movements, and body position can influence a person's response to a speaker. Do the individuals who speak a different language or come from a different culture understand the presentation? Do they seem to agree with what is being said? Many studies have shown that being able to view the person who is talking aids both understanding and credibility.

© Photodisc/Getty Images, Inc.

Figure 3-3: Videoconferencing allows for valuable nonverbal communication.

Activity 3-1: Planning a Videoconference

As the technology assistant for a large manufacturing company in Chicago, you have been assigned the task of arranging a videoconference between the robotics teams in Chicago and Albuquerque. Write a list of information you will need before you can effectively plan the conference.

_____

_____

_____

_____

_____

_____

_____

_____

_____

Activity 3-2: Scheduling a Videoconference

Assume that you have been asked to organize a two-hour videoconference that will originate in New York City and have other participants in Paris, France; Osaka, Japan; Miami, Florida; Caracas, Venezuela; Honolulu, Hawaii; Dallas, Texas; and Stockholm, Sweden. Considering the time differences, what time should the conference be held in New York? Use the time zone map on page 26 or web sites on page 27 to help with your decision.

Time conference should be held in New York City: _____

_____

Audience, Location, and Timing

Activity 3-3: Understanding Time Zones

Using the start time you established in Activity 3-2 for the meeting in New York City, what will be the start time in the other cities where the videoconference will be held?

City	Start Time
Paris, France	_____
Osaka, Japan	_____
Miami, Florida	_____
Caracas, Venezuela	_____
Dallas, Texas	_____
Honolulu, Hawaii	_____
Stockholm, Sweden	_____

Activity 3-4: Identifying Cultural Differences

Since five countries will be represented at the conference described in Activity 3-2, what recommendations can you make to the speaker so the presentation will be easier to understand by all attending?

_____

_____

_____

_____

_____

4 Assigning Responsibilities

Focus

"Poor videoconferences cost your company money, while good videoconferences can add to its profits."

—Julian Goldstein & Jeremy Goldstein
in *Videoconferencing Secrets*

Announcements of a Videoconference

Why is the title of this section plural? Isn't one announcement regarding a meeting sufficient? Generally, the answer is, "No." Busy schedules and forgetfulness often make it necessary to provide multiple reminders of upcoming events. Two or three such reminders usually are sufficient.

The initial announcement of a videoconference should be sent out as soon as a date and theme are set, so participants can schedule their time to attend. This first announcement is usually sent by e-mail or facsimile. It should be short and to the point, advising Who? What? When? and Where? Be sure to announce both a date and a day of the week. Since most videoconferences involve multiple time zones, provide the specific time of the conference in each zone. Some videoconference leaders give the time zone conversion to all the participants.

A follow-up announcement should be sent several days before the videoconference. It should include the meeting agenda plus an expanded version of the information provided earlier. Use this opportunity to address any inquiries or confusion that may have resulted from the first announcement.

Send a final reminder announcement on the day prior to, or even a few hours prior to, the actual start of the videoconference. It can contain any last minute changes that may have become necessary, such as the addition of more videoconference sites to the meeting.

Figure 4-1: **Reminder announcements about upcoming videoconferences are critical.**

Confirmations

Have you ever heard the expression that the only real disasters are the ones you don't expect? This adage applies to videoconferences also. Using confirmations will help avoid some meeting disasters.

Confirm all details with the videoconference network or site coordinator several days or hours before the meeting. Make sure the meeting is scheduled to start as planned. Include the following items in the confirmation:

1. The specific sites involved

2. The start and end times

3. All visual aid requirements

4. Any special needs of the session

5. Phone numbers and contact information for all participants and coordinators

Tip

Be sure to bring your confirmation forms with you to your meeting. They will have all the necessary phone numbers in case there is a problem.

Confirm arrangements with the participants. Make sure they received the announcement, a copy of the agenda, and other materials such as presentation slides that were sent to them in advance. If they are presenting during the session, try to get a copy of their slides so that the slides can be reviewed to make sure they fit the proper TV format.

Agenda Use

One of the most important parts of planning any meeting, but especially a video-conference, is developing an **agenda,** a list of topics to be discussed or order of business to be followed in a meeting. Some companies and universities consider an agenda so essential that they do not permit a meeting to be announced unless an agenda is provided.

In a videoconference, special steps can be taken in preparing the agenda. First, limit the number of items to be discussed to the top three. In a typical videoconference time span of two hours, a maximum of three topics can be adequately handled. Save additional items for future videoconferences. Keep the topic items brief, concise, and to the point. Use sentence fragments to keep each agenda item to one line. If more information needs to be provided regarding the discussion topics, handle the information in a separate document.

Print the agenda in large format and bold type, and eliminate all footnotes. Anything printed in standard text size and unbolded will be unreadable in a videoconference. Be sure to save the text for the day of the event. Watch a normal television advertisement to get an idea of how bold an agenda should be. Notice how much larger the text in the advertisement appears than the text on your PC or laptop. (That's because the TV screen has less resolution and the viewer sits further away from it than a computer.) For a quick test, print an agenda on a piece of paper, then drop it on the floor. If you can still read the agenda while standing up, it is probably large and bold enough to be seen by participants on their TVs.

Also show an agenda on a slide at the start of the videoconference session, and again following breaks. This brings participants back on track. Make sure the agenda can be seen clearly on a TV screen as shown in Figure 4-2. Experts recommend the following formatting guidelines:

■ Always use Arial bold font in 24 point or larger size. Tests have shown this to be an easily readable format for viewing on a TV screen.

■ Use landscape orientation with wide side margins to avoid the text being cut off.

■ Do not be afraid to make the text bold and large. *Remember: in most videoconferences, the screen resolution is less than that of a normal TV because of the image compression.*

Send the agenda with the announcement of the meeting. If this is not possible, send the agenda out at least several days in advance of the videoconference. Since you may be dealing with many different time zones, the beginning of the day in one location may be after the end of others' workdays. In this case, they will not see the agenda until the next day. If the next day happens to fall on a weekend, they may not see the agenda until the next week. Sending an agenda early is important because participants need notice of the topics to be discussed in the videoconference. Otherwise, they may not be adequately prepared to discuss the agenda items in an informed manner. The participants may also need time to develop their own videoconference slides, if they are presenting.

Planning Meeting Agenda

Conference Room C   April 20, 200x

Welcome & introductions (10 minutes)
    Sophie Carroll

I. **Review of accomplishments (30 minutes)**
    All managers

II. **Proposed budget for next year (20 minutes)**
    Juan Menendez

III. **Goals for next six months (1 hour)**
    All managers

Figure 4-2: Videoconference agenda slide format

Assigning Responsibilities

Note Taking and Taping

Minutes of some videoconference meetings are taken, typed, and distributed to the participants at a later date. Minutes or notes are especially important if the subject is controversial or if participants are expected to take action later. Other reasons for note taking at a videoconference should also be considered:

■ All participants may not be in the room at all times.

■ Some participants may have trouble hearing everything that is said.

■ Participants may disagree on specific points that are made.

■ The company or organization wants a record of what is covered.

To reduce the chance of making a mistake when compiling notes after the videoconference, be sure that the meeting is recorded. When making the reservation for the videoconference, and again several hours before the actual start time, ask the videoconference site coordinator or network coordinator to arrange to have the session recorded. Ask for a confirmation that recording will occur.

Specify exactly which video you wish to have recorded, either OUTGOING video or INCOMING. Older networks use a videocassette recorder (VCR) to handle the recording, while newer videoconference networks may "burn" a DVD recording. They may also archive the session by converting the video to Internet protocol (IP) format and storing it on a server for later retrieval. When using IP, be certain to obtain the web address (URL) of the storage and ask for what period it will be stored.

The chairperson of a videoconference should never take the notes for a conference. Always locate another participant to handle the task of recording the minutes. It is difficult to simultaneously lead the discussion and accurately record exactly who said what.

Despite all the hype about "the paperless office," most companies are about as dependent on paper as ever. Although the meeting agenda may have been sent to all participants via e-mail, a printed copy

© Photodisc/Getty Images, Inc.

Figure 4-3: Assign one participant the important task of taking thorough notes.

should also be provided to each participant. A courtesy copy should be e-mailed to the videoconference network or site coordinator.

Some participants may wish to take their own notes using a laptop PC or a PDA such as a Palm®. Other participants may bring cell phones into the videoconference. Ask all participants to keep their screens or flashing lights away from the videoconference cameras. The screens and flashing lights from electronic devices may seriously degrade the videoconference video.

Some presenters are willing to provide the slides of their presentation in advance of the videoconference. If so, send the slides to all participants via e-mail or facsimile as early as possible. This gives the participants time to study the material in advance of the session and to prepare for the discussion. It is also desirable to have the actual slides made into hard copy for distribution at all the videoconference sites. This gives the participants a handy paper on which to take notes.

© Photodisc/Getty Images, Inc.

Figure 4-4: Be sure all screens and flashing lights are facing away from videoconference cameras.

Follow-Up

The chairperson or leader of the videoconference meeting is not finished when the meeting is over. Action items that came up during the meeting must be immediately addressed. If participants agree to handle any items and fail to do so, the chairperson must follow up with them. If a follow-up videoconference will be held, note the action items on the announcement or agenda for the next videoconference. For example: "Manuel Rodriguez will discuss the results of his research described at the last meeting."

Activity 4-4: Taking Notes

Watch a thirty-minute television show on any subject and also record the show on VCR for later viewing. Take notes during the show and write the most important points on the lines below. Watch the show again several hours or a day or two later. Using a colored pen, add any points you missed in your first round of note taking. Analyze your final notes and summarize what you learned from the two-part process of note taking.

_____

_____

_____

_____

_____

_____

_____

5 Managing Videoconferences

Focus

"You know that preparation is important to any meeting's success. And you prepare for a videoconference in the same ways you prepare for any meeting. . . ."

—PictureTel Corporation
Power User's Guide to Videoconferencing

External Challenges

What happens when you are not in charge of the videoconference schedule? Say, for example, an important customer wants a sales meeting on a specific date, but your budget won't allow you to fly all the necessary technical and marketing personnel to the customer's office. Videoconferencing can come to your rescue. With both private and public videoconference rooms available in every major city throughout the world, you can bring the customer to the company when you can't send the company to the customer.

To set up a conference, contact your company's videoconference network coordinator and describe the videoconferencing needs. If the company does not have a videoconferencing system or has a system but not a central manager, then what?

Solve the problem by contacting a public videoconference network coordinator such as Sprint Video Conferencing^{SM}, V-Span®, AT&T TeleConference Systems, Wire One Glowpoint^{TM}, or other major telecommunications or telephone companies. They can quickly put you in touch with their videoconference network experts who can guide you through the process of setting up the meeting.

Internal Schedules

Setting up a meeting for company employees who will present at the videoconference for a customer requires detailed planning. In many ways, internal scheduling is easier than external coordination because the customer requested the conference. Staff members are expected to present or participate as a part of their jobs.

A Step-by-Step Plan

After an announcement of the videoconference is sent (Lesson 4), quickly verify that the intended participants received it. When most of the internal guest speakers have confirmed their presence, contact each one individually:

- Verify the date, time, and the person's availability for the videoconference.

- Review the time zone differences to reduce the risk of timing difficulties.

- Explain how the videoconference will flow and what will be expected of speakers. This is especially important if speakers have limited experience with videoconferencing.

- Provide directions to the videoconference site, especially if it is in a public facility away from the company offices or if they must travel at night to get to it.

- Assign each speaker a contact at the site and provide the contact's telephone number.

- Give directions for preparing slides if speakers plan to present slides.

- Send a follow-up announcement shortly before the videoconference. Verify that it was received by all speakers, and then confirm that no last-minute changes have occurred in the speakers' plans and that the speakers understand the agenda and the meeting script.

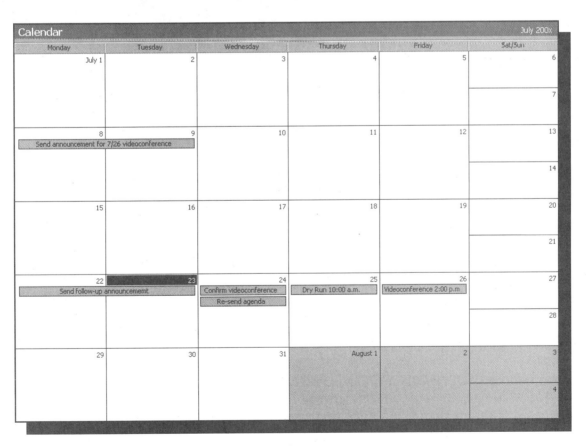

Figure 5-1: Calendar of videoconference events

The Script

The meeting script is a brief plan of who does what at a videoconference and when they do it. It usually is not shared with the customer or other external participants. The script should specify the time limit for each part of the videoconference. For example, a speaker may have 10 minutes to present his or her slides and then another 5 minutes to handle questions from the customer. If the question and answer period (Q&A) is not needed, the presenter passes the videoconference over to the next speaker.

If, on the other hand, the customer asks the speaker several questions and the speaker's allotted time is limited, a plan must be in place to handle the situation. One method is for the current speaker to suggest that additional questions will be addressed by an upcoming speaker. In this case, the current speaker should also volunteer to be available after the conference to meet with the customer. The goal is to manage time so that the videoconference does not end abruptly because network connection time is over.

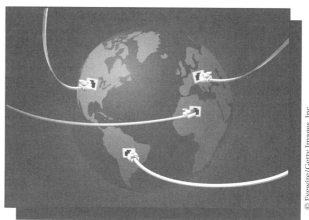

Figure 5-2: **Videoconferencing services are available worldwide.**

Distribution of Videoconference Services

Despite the best efforts of everyone involved, one or more important presenters may not have access to a videoconference room. In such cases, you may:

■ Arrange for a substitute presenter.

■ Ask the network coordinator to provide a dial-in telephone port for the speaker. Then as the speaker discusses each slide over the phone, the meeting host can change the slides on the videoconference screen.

Assuring Equipment Success

Once all details with speakers and presenters are handled, it's time for a test session to verify that all the equipment is operational and meets expectations. Short videoconference sessions of 15 to 30 minutes should be held for the purpose of checking equipment operation and interconnection, listening to audio, and viewing video. Few or no participants should be present.

For a customer-requested videoconference, a "dry run," or practice session, is recommended. This session involves most or all of the company participants who will attend the actual session, and the purpose is to "get all the bugs out." The length of the practice videoconference session may be as long or longer than the actual session. Each presenter will display and briefly describe the slides to be used in his or her presentation and show how the presentation will transition into the next topic of the presentation.

User Instructions

During the practice session, the presenters may need to be coached, since this may be the first videoconference for some. Others may have experienced a videoconference, but never looked at their presentation from the customer's perspective. Whatever the case, several potential problems should be addressed:

1. **Too many slides to show.** Often speakers try to crowd too much information into their presentations. For example, if a presenter is allocated 20 minutes of the overall videoconference session, only about 20 slides can be used successfully. Even that number—one per minute—does not allow for interaction, questions, and unexpected delays. Five to ten slides are more appropriate.

2. **Poorly designed slides.** Remember the function of the CODEC? The CODEC compresses videoconference images for transmission over special digital telephone lines. This means that PC video and videoconference video are not the same. Slide type that looks perfectly readable on a PC screen may be too small to be read in a videoconference, and a color that appears adequate on a PC screen may cause distortion when displayed on a TV screen in a videoconference. Some of these difficulties may not be detected until the slides are actually transmitted; that is another reason why practice videoconference sessions are helpful.

Figure 5-3: Well-designed and poorly-designed slides

3. **No camera control.** Hosts in remote videoconference rooms may have little or no experience with cameras. They may show an entire table of individuals targeted by the system's default camera position—the zoom OUT position—during the entire conference. This view does not allow for the intimate interaction that a videoconference can provide when the presenter's face is clearly seen. The camera at each site should be on zoom IN so a close up view of each speaker can be seen. Watch a news program on TV and notice how the speakers are given a head and shoulders camera shot. This same camera shot is important for a speaker in a videoconference.

4. **Poor audio.** This condition most often results from a number of factors:

   ■ Participants fail to mute their microphones when they are not presenting.

   ■ The speaker is located too far away from the microphone.

   ■ Incoming audio volume for the conference is turned up too high. This usually results in a long delayed echo, which can be severely distracting to all.

   ■ The room is poorly designed and has weak acoustical properties. Providing lapel microphones for the speakers may solve the problem.

Tip

Avoid making distracting sounds, such as tapping a pencil, shuffling papers, or twisting in a chair. The microphone is sensitive, and any noise made at one site could be amplified at the other locations.

Managing Videoconferences

Activity 5-1: Using Public Networks

 Log onto the Internet and search for information about the public videoconference networks mentioned in this lesson. Write a summary of what you learned.

Network	Types of Services Offered	Restrictions
Sprint Video Conferencing^{SM} www.sprintbiz.com		
V-Span® www.vspan.com		
AT&T TeleConference Services www.att.com/conferencing		
Wire One Glowpoint™ www.wireone.com		

Activity 5-2: Preparing a Script

Prepare a script or plan for the videoconference described below. Indicate the amount of time you will give to each speaker and the points you will want each speaker to cover.

A one and one-half hour videoconference will be held with a customer who is interested in purchasing 50,000 of your company's new remote-controlled toy trucks to stock in her stores for the upcoming holiday season. The customer asks you to cover the following topics in the meeting:

■ Why you think the truck will be a popular gift item

■ The special features of the truck

■ The quality of construction

■ The type of advertising assistance you will provide

■ The delivery schedule

■ Your payment plan

■ Your return policy

You have asked the following individuals from your company to participate: sales manager, manufacturing manager, advertising manager, shipping manager, accounting supervisor, and customer service manager.

_____

_____

_____

_____

_____

_____

_____

Managing Videoconferences

Activity 5-3: Training Presenters

Assume that none of the presenters nor the camera operator in Activity 5-2 has previous experience with a videoconference. Prepare a list of recommendations that will make the conference more successful.

1. _____

_____

2. _____

_____

3. _____

_____

4. _____

_____

5. _____

_____

6. _____

_____

7. _____

_____

8. _____

_____

9. _____

_____

10. _____

_____

6 Creating Slides, Visual Aids, and Handouts

Focus

"Design your PowerPoint videoconference slides to look good and to be readable on screen. Remember, test your slides on the videoconference system in time to fix any problems."

—Jamie Poindexter, Manager Teleconference Operations
University of Wisconsin–Extension

General Slide Format and Fonts

One of the most frustrating and disappointing experiences in viewing any videoconference is the inability to see the slides or other visuals. Imagine driving 50 miles to view a special presentation, then finding that the words on the charts and slides are too small to see. This is similar to attending a music concert where the volume is so low you can't hear the songs—you probably would ask for a concert refund. Yet, time after time, videoconference presenters show bad visuals without a second thought. Don't make that mistake yourself.

The most common method of showing a visual aid at a videoconference is to print the slide material on a **graphics camera.** This is a special TV camera with a short focal length lens that points straight down to the conference table surface. The camera serves the same purpose as the overhead projector that speakers use for their clear plastic slides in a conventional presentation. Most videoconference rooms are equipped with a graphics camera. Some are table mounted, others are ceiling mounted.

Another method—one that replaces both graphics cameras and overhead projection systems—is an electronic interface between a PC or laptop and the videoconference system. A device called a **scan converter** changes the PC image of the slide to a TV image.

Most presenters use a presentation graphics program such as Microsoft PowerPoint® to create their videoconference slides. If you don't have

Figure 6-1: A scan converter changes a PC image to a TV image for a videoconference slide.

access to PowerPoint®, use a public computer at the library in your town. A sample slide is shown in Figure 6-2. Follow these instructions for using PowerPoint®:

- Create a new file, then select a template style. PowerPoint® offers several useful templates for creating slides. Select one that has a clean and uncluttered appearance.

- Use Arial font of at least 24 point for easy readability.

- Use boldface black text for main points. Refrain from shadowing, as shadowing reduces readability.

- Use landscape orientation (sideways).

- Use consistent punctuation, spelling, and abbreviations.

- Avoid wordiness.

- Eliminate visuals that are too small to be seen by everyone.

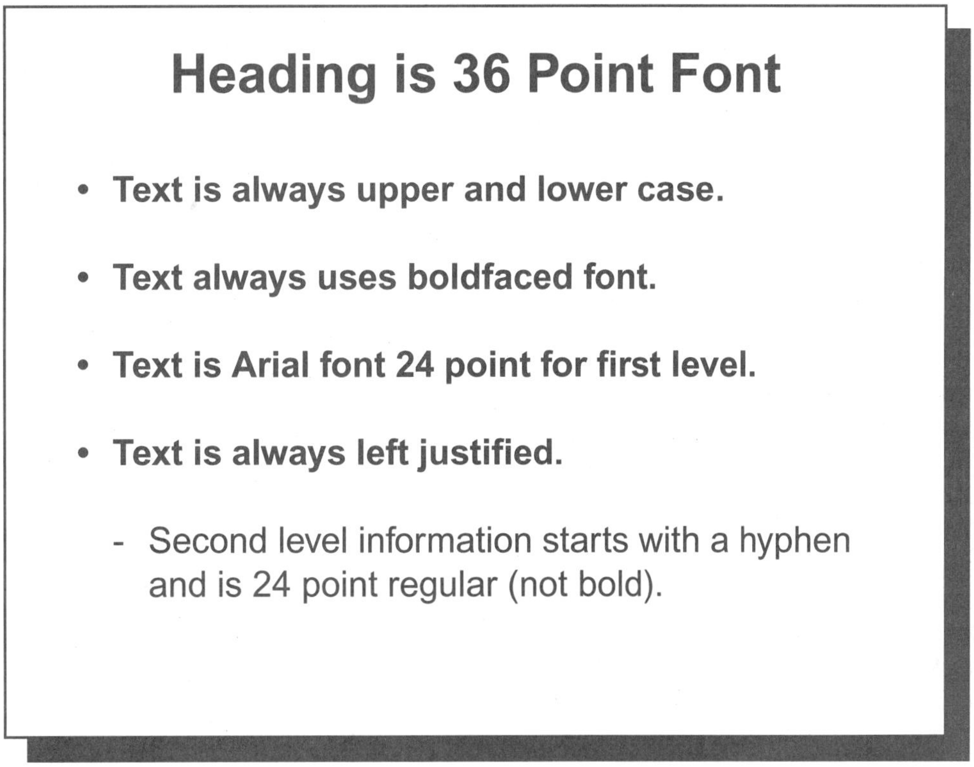

Heading is 36 Point Font

- **Text is always upper and lower case.**

- **Text always uses boldfaced font.**

- **Text is Arial font 24 point for first level.**

- **Text is always left justified.**

    - Second level information starts with a hyphen and is 24 point regular (not bold).

Figure 6-2: Proper videoconference slide formatting

Viewing Range

What is normal viewing distance from a videoconference screen? Sit too close to the TV and the image will look grainy. Sit too far away, and the graphics will be difficult to read or interpret. Good viewing distance can be anywhere from $2\times$ the diagonal size of the TV to $9\times$ as much.

Suppose you're watching a 36-inch TV screen, which is the most common-sized TV screen used in videoconference rooms. The closest you should sit to the screen is about 6 feet ($2 \times 36" = 72" = 6$ feet). The farthest you should sit is about 27 feet ($9 \times 36" = 324" = 27$ feet). This long distance works if you are watching a talking-head type of presentation. If any text visual aids are used, the maximum distance should be reduced to about $6\times$, or about 18 feet.

Establishing appropriate viewing range is the reason many videoconference rooms measure approximately 20 feet $\times$ 20 feet. This size allows enough room for the video-conference equipment to be placed against a wall at one end of the room while also accommodating a practical number of participants. Make sure the room is not taken up by a large conference table that reduces the space for viewers.

Charts and Graphs

Use the same guidelines for making slides that show charts or graphs. If charts contain columns of data and you expect your audience to read those columns, the information must be at least Arial 24 point. If that format takes up too much space, condense the chart to fewer columns or present the chart in multiple parts using several slides.

Figure 6-3 demonstrates an acceptable format for viewing a graph.

Whether you use solid, dashed, or other line designs in graphs, use a bold font for the lines so they can be easily seen. Keep in mind that the vertical and horizontal axis titles must be readable, and the gradations must be visible. If a graph is too large for showing detail, provide a zoomed-in or enlarged image of the portion of the graph that you are discussing or showing.

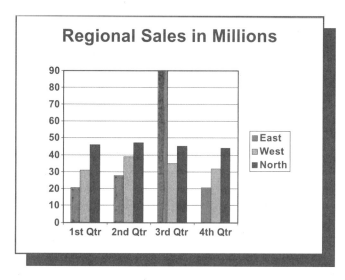

Figure 6-3: Sample bar graph for videoconference slide

Creating Slides, Visual Aids, and Handouts

Creating Tables

Printed tables that contain a great deal of information can cause problems in a video-conference. Here are several approaches to presenting tables:

■ Display the entire table with specific data shown in color. Quickly switch from the full table to a slide that enlarges or highlights the colored data. The audience will realize that the material being discussed is taken from a larger document. Figures 6-4 and 6-5 demonstrate how this process works.

■ Use a large wall screen projector to display the table. Turn the projector off during the remainder of the presentation unless you will be referring to the table. Otherwise, viewers may be distracted.

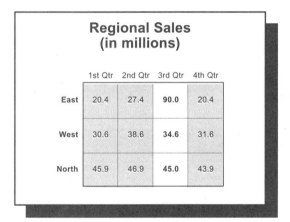

Figure 6-4: Sample table for videoconference slide

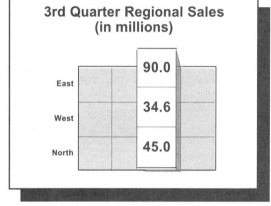

Figure 6-5: Sample table with specific data from larger table

■ Consider providing a network connected PC to each pair of participants in the videoconference room, or ask the participants to bring their own laptops. Send the table to be viewed over the network directly to the computer users' links.

■ Use a more conventional method by having the table printed cleanly and clearly on paper. Ask an associate in each videoconference room to pass the table out to the participants at the appropriate point in your presentation.

Use of Color and Special Effects

Have you ever noticed how a color viewed on your PC sometimes looks different when it's printed? The same difference can occur when translating between the **chroma,** or color scheme, used in a PC and the chroma seen on a videoconference television. Some colors simply do not translate well. This is called the **magenta effect** because of the color blending or chroma distortion that often takes place. To reduce color problems consider the following recommendations:

■ Avoid the use of bright reds (which tend to "flare"), pale yellows (which tend to "wash out"), and some blues (which fade into the background) in charts and on slides.

■ Use colors sparingly and only when truly necessary. Having each letter of text a different color may look striking, but it also makes the message difficult to read.

■ Use colors for contrast or emphasis only when color really is necessary. Just making the text larger often can achieve the same result.

■ Avoid the use of wildly different colors for contrast.

Always test color slides for compatibility before using them. Make certain you are previewing the slides after they have come through the CODEC process—called a **loop-back.** Using this method, you can also check to see how well the average participant in far away cities can read the materials.

Tip

According to AT&T TeleConference Services, videoconference planners should follow these guidelines for successful presentation slides:

■ Use a bold typeface of 24 points or larger.

■ Use only two-thirds of an 8½ × 11" page, leaving the margins free.

■ Use landscape orientation.

■ Keep pictures simple and words brief. Use only graphics that are easy to understand, such as simple bar charts, pie charts, and tables.

Designing Handouts

By this time, you may be thinking that using handouts is unnecessary because the participants have seen and heard you and viewed all your materials on screen. However, people often like to take notes during a presentation. What better way to do that than on your handout materials?

Types of Handouts

The simplest type of handout is a paper copy of the slides used in the presentation. Ask an associate to distribute the handouts to each participant. In addition to the slides, the handouts should contain a cover page with the presentation title and speaker's name plus perhaps one or two more blank pages for note taking.

If you wish to provide an article or document for background reading, distribute it before the conference by e-mail or fax, or hand it out after the videoconference is over. Handing out an article at the beginning of your presentation tempts the participants to read the article when you want them to pay attention to what you are saying.

Delivery, Distribution, and Timing

The most efficient way to distribute handouts is to send them by e-mail over the datacom network to each site. They also can be printed and sent by fax or postal delivery. Request the site coordinator to copy and distribute them to participants.

Timing of the distribution of handouts is critical for maximum videoconference effectiveness. Ideally, you should distribute the slides with the first announcement of the conference so participants have the longest opportunity to prepare. If this is not possible, the slides should be sent with the last follow-up announcement (often the third or fourth announcement). Have extra sets of handouts available in the videoconference room at the start of the session.

Activity 6-1: Creating Slides

Using PowerPoint® or a word processing program, create the following slides for use in a videoconference presentation. Condense the words to a minimum, and format the slides so they will be easy to read and attractive.

Slide 1

The top ten challenges many small business owners face are getting new customers, retaining customers, marketing, networking, developing the business, motivating employees, increasing sales, providing leadership, team building, and managing time.

Slide 2

Number of small businesses identifying top concerns

1 = No problem; 2 = Small problem; 3 = Neither big nor small problem;
4 = Somewhat big problem; 5 = Biggest problem

Getting new customers	1 = 32	2 = 4	3 = 14	4 = 26	5 = 135
Retaining customers	1 = 52	2 = 16	3 = 34	4 = 30	5 = 76
Marketing	1 = 50	2 = 15	3 = 34	4 = 43	5 = 68
Networking	1 = 44	2 = 16	3 = 41	4 = 41	5 = 65
Developing the business	1 = 44	2 = 12	3 = 46	4 = 48	5 = 58
Motivating employees	1 = 54	2 = 14	3 = 38	4 = 49	5 = 58
Increasing sales	1 = 62	2 = 21	3 = 43	4 = 26	5 = 56
Providing leadership	1 = 62	2 = 13	3 = 39	4 = 46	5 = 54
Team building	1 = 64	2 = 20	3 = 39	4 = 37	5 = 53
Managing time	1 = 63	2 = 14	3 = 41	4 = 42	5 = 53

Creating Slides, Visual Aids, and Handouts

Slide 3

Technology training seen by small business owners as very important for their staffs and reported in a survey of 230 businesses

Computer skills	40%
e-commerce	41%
Digital marketing	32%
Presentation software	21%
New products	16%
Certification or licensing	7%

Activity 6-2: Adding Color

Using the slides you created in Activity 1, add appropriate color to highlight specific sections you want participants to observe.

Activity 6-3: Recommending Viewing Range

What do you recommend as the maximum viewing range from the TV screen for each TV identified below?

TV Screen Size	Maximum Viewing Range for Talking Head Presentation	Maximum Viewing Range for Text/Visual Presentation
52"		
32"		
29"		
24"		
20"		

Creating Slides, Visual Aids, and Handouts

Activity 6-4: Making a Recommendation

Formulate a list of guidelines for the presenter described in the case below.

The accountant for a large manufacturing company plans to present the company's annual budget by videoconference to the senior vice presidents who head up divisions around the country. He has many slides of charts with figures and has been given a brief period of time for his portion of the presentation. Prepare a presentation plan that will include the following:

1. How the slides can be presented most efficiently

2. How color should be used

3. What handouts to provide

4. How handouts should be distributed and on what schedule.

Presentation Plan:

_____

_____

_____

_____

_____

_____

_____

_____

_____

_____

7 Equipment, Systems, and Network

Focus

"Watching a technician who's trying to get your videoconferencing gear to work properly is much less stressful than watching an airline mechanic trying to fix the plane you're on."

—Fred S. Knight, Editor/Publisher
Business Communications Review

Audio Systems

Successful videoconferencing occurs when remote participants and on-site participants feel as if they are actually in the room together. One of the best ways to achieve this feeling, known as presence, is through the audio system. While video doesn't have to be perfect in a videoconference, problems occur when the sound is distorted by an echo, a reverberation, or some other undesired effect. An old expression in videoconferencing states, "Lose the video and we talk. Lose the audio and we walk."

How can you tell if a videoconference room needs sound treatment? Try this easy test: Does the room sound different when it is full of people? Since bodies are mostly water, they are excellent sound absorbers. If you can detect a sound difference when a room is empty of people, the room probably needs some type of additional acoustical treatment. Several common sources for audio problems can be easily identified and addressed.

The Speakers

The speakers in a TV set, even in the most expensive models, are poor performers when it comes to creating presence in a videoconference. Yet, many low cost or portable videoconferencing systems use only the TV speakers for **audio output,** or sound production. While participants may be able to hear a newscast clearly in spite of poor TV speakers, their small size, limited frequency range, non-responsiveness, or placement in a cabinet reduces presence.

By replacing the internal TV speakers with a pair of low cost, external high fidelity stereo speakers from a local electronics store, you can significantly improve the audio quality in a videoconference room. This is similar to improving the sound quality of a PC by adding small external speakers.

The Videoconference Room Design

Videoconference systems are often portable so they can be moved from conference room to conference room. These systems produce a good sound when used in well-designed rooms that contain acoustical tiles or panels, carpeted floors, and padded furniture for absorbing errant sounds. These features give the room a suitable sound quality—what professionals call an acoustically dead room. However, if a videoconference room is not well designed for sound, the audio quality can be affected. For example, large glass panels or several windows along a wall can create distracting sound reflections.

How can room problems be corrected? First, try closing the drapes or lowering the blinds. If the videoconference system can be moved within the room, place it in a different location, so its speakers project away from the glass panels. If lead time permits, paint the walls with a rough textured paint or install heavy flocked wallpaper on all the walls. This is called wall carpeting. In severe cases, install floor carpeting on one or more walls to dampen the distracting reflections.

Figure 7-1: Typical conference room

Microphones

Unlike TV, videoconferencing is a two-way medium, so the quality of the microphones is important. If the sound quality is poor, improper placement of the microphones may be the culprit. If the presenters are too far away from the nearest microphone, they will sound to remote listeners like they're speaking from the bottom of a deep well. If they are too close to the microphone, their voices may boom or sound distorted. If they move books near the microphone, muffled sounds may be heard at the far end. If they shuffle papers, a crashing sound may be heard.

Figure 7-2: With a proper microphone, a participant should be able to speak in a normal voice tone and volume.

In a properly outfitted videoconference room, all presenters or participants should be able to speak in a normal voice tone and volume while still being heard clearly at all video-conference sites. Pre-session testing should detect any problems and allow time for corrections. In some cases, the main presenter may need to use an additional lapel microphone. That should be a last resort because it may produce unnatural fidelity. Remember: any sites not actively participating in a discussion should mute or silence their microphones to prevent the pickup of potentially embarrassing side conversations and other distracting sounds.

Long-Delayed Echo

If a microphone at one site is too close to the audio output speakers, it may pick up the output of the speakers and re-send the sound through the videoconference network. This causes a low-level, long-delayed echo that distracts the speaker. Some speakers, upon hearing the sound of their own voice after a second or so of delay, become so distracted they cannot speak until the echo is corrected. The easy solution is to ask the offending videoconference site to turn down the sound volume coming from the speakers until the long-delayed echo disappears.

Video Systems

Camera operators frequently fail to control their motion cameras adequately. Even though videoconferencing systems usually come with at least one robotically controlled, auto-focus camera, mistakes can occur.

A videoconference camera often displays a **default shot,** an image of the videoconference room that is shown throughout the entire session. Usually, this is a long-range, wide-angle view of the room. Though all participants in the room can be seen by remote viewers, the viewers may have trouble determining who is talking. Even if they recognize the voice of the speaker, they will see only a few facial features, expressions, and gestures. This is similar to talking with someone in a normal tone of voice while standing on the opposite side of a large parking lot.

Figure 7-3: This seating arrangement is not appropriate for a videoconference and would make camera operation extremely difficult.

The problem can be corrected if the videoconference camera is **zoomed** in, that is, extended for a close-up view of the current speaker. This can be a head and shoulders view, or it can be closer if needed.

Modern videoconference systems come with memories that store several robotically controlled motion camera positions. These remembered or stored camera positions are called **pre-sets** and can be very helpful in assuring consistent viewing.

Operating the Camera

Before a videoconference begins, move the robotic motion camera's pointing position to the person sitting in Chair No. 1 at the conference table, and then store this position in Pre-set No. 1. Continue doing this until the chair positions of all the main presenters are stored in their own pre-set. Then, when each person talks, the individual controlling the camera can push a single button so that the camera zooms to the speaker and auto-focuses on his or her specific image.

Exterior windows allow enormous amounts of natural light to enter a room. While human eyes normally adjust to this lighting after a few minutes, the motion video videoconference camera does not have the same adjustment capability. If the camera is allowed to view a window, the auto shutter closes down significantly and the room looks like the inside of a cave. To solve this problem, draw the blinds over the windows, point the camera away from the windows, or use a room without windows.

Figure 7-4: **Camera controls can be pre-set to focus on individual participants.**

Tip

When focusing a camera on an individual, remember that a person's image looks best when seen from the waist up, with about 10 percent of the picture area left above his or her head. If you'll need to focus on different groups of people during a videoconference, use pre-sets to create up to four views or segments of the room. During the conference, simply press one of your pre-set buttons to move the camera instead of trying to manually pan and zoom, which can be cumbersome.

Clothing and Backgrounds

Participants in a videoconference should wear solid color shirts or blouses that are light blue, gray or earth tones. Other colors, especially bright red or bright white, may make the clothing seem battery powered. Avoid stripes and patterned clothing that can seem to vibrate in video.

Don't forget the wall that's behind the speakers. Most conference rooms are painted a soft off-white color, which appears pale yellow to a videoconference camera. Most everything else the camera includes in the wall shot will also look yellow. The wall behind participants should be a flat, medium blue or gray color for best contrast. At the least, temporarily remove any artwork, photographs, or other designs on the wall. These complex images make the CODEC work harder, which further degrades the image clarity and motion of the participants.

Control Systems

Before a videoconference, familiarize yourself with the remote or console device that operates the CODEC. This device also controls the camera position and audio volume. Ask for a demonstration of its use and get answers to any questions you may have. Test the device before you use it. If possible, practice with the controls until they feel natural. This will reduce fumbling and give you confidence while you are conducting the actual session.

Figure 7-5: A remote control or console device allows users to place calls, adjust volume, and pan or zoom the camera.

Peripheral Equipment

In addition to audio, video, and control systems, most videoconference systems are equipped with several other devices. One of the more common is a videocassette recorder (VCR) that records either the outgoing or the incoming video. Though a VCR can be switched back and forth to record, it will not be able to record both incoming and outgoing images at the same time. Even if the actual meeting is not recorded, a VCR can be helpful during the test session. Use it to record the outgoing video so you can view how others will see your site. Watch the tape recording several times so you will be better prepared for the actual meeting.

The test session is also a good time to become familiar with how scan converters change PC images to TV format. During the test, you can view the slides or other objects you wish to present. This is the time to determine if any changes are needed to improve clarity.

Take-Along Equipment

A presenter normally takes the same things to a videoconference as he or she would take to any other meeting, including note pads, pager, cell phone, or a PDA. When you use a laptop computer to display slides, two additional steps are needed.

■ Determine during the test session if the videoconference scan converter is compatible with your laptop.

■ Take along the laptop battery charger so the laptop internal battery doesn't fail in the middle of a presentation.

Two connections are needed for the laptop—AC power and the video output port. Make certain the battery charger power cord reaches the AC power outlet. Some videoconference rooms have an outlet on the conference table, but others have only wall outlets. The connection to the video output port is usually on the conference table too, but don't count on that. You may need a special extension cable.

Finally, if you need to connect to the local area network (LAN) to retrieve presentation slides, e-mail, or other data, make certain the videoconference room has a LAN connection and that its cable reaches the laptop on the conference table. This is especially important if you are planning to conduct a simultaneous **dataconference**, such as Microsoft NetMeeting®, with the other videoconference participants. In addition to communicating with audio and video, a dataconference allows participants to exchange graphics, transfer files, and use a text-based chat program.

Activity 7-1: Correcting Audio Problems

After the last two meetings held in a videoconference room you manage, participants have complained to you about being unable to hear the speakers. Prepare a checklist of the items you should examine in order to correct the problem.

Checklist for Correcting Audio Problems

✓ _____

✓ _____

✓ _____

✓ _____

✓ _____

✓ _____

✓ _____

✓ _____

✓ _____

✓ _____

✓ _____

✓ _____

✓ _____

Equipment, Systems, and Network

Activity 7-2: Capitalizing on Presence

As the manager of the videoconference center at a large pharmaceutical company, you've been concerned about the lack of presence during meetings. Many of the speakers at your videoconferences don't understand why they have to worry about presence. Write an e-mail memo describing presence; identify why it is important to conferences; and give instructions to speakers on how they can improve presence.

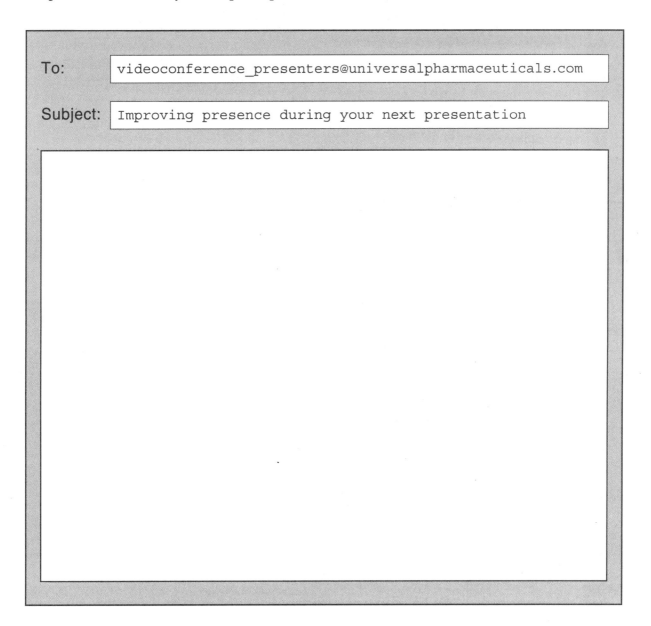

To: videoconference_presenters@universalpharmaceuticals.com

Subject: Improving presence during your next presentation

Equipment, Systems, and Network

Activity 7-3: Improving the View

In past videoconferences, you've noticed that the view seen by observers is often of a room instead of a speaker; color sometimes is distorted; and patches of black occur during which the speaker can be heard but not seen. Occasionally, the person shown on camera is not the person speaking, or the view of the person is so far away that facial expressions cannot be seen. What recommendations would you make for improving the video?

Improving Video

Problem   **Recommended Correction**

1. View is of a room, although a person is   _____
   speaking.   _____
                                                  _____

2. Everything looks pale yellow.   _____
                                                  _____
                                                  _____

3. The scene goes black.   _____
                                                  _____
                                                  _____

4. One person speaks, but another's face   _____
   is shown.   _____
                                                  _____

5. The speaker's full body is shown, but facial _____
   expressions and gestures can't be seen.   _____
                                                  _____

Equipment, Systems, and Network

Activity 7-4: Upgrading the Videoconference Room

A videoconference room used by the industrial waste company where you work is described below. Presenters often complain that the room is unsuitable. Analyze what is wrong with the room and describe what should be done to improve it for videoconferencing. If something other than the room appears to be a problem, identify the issue and suggest how to correct it.

Description of Room, Viewing, and Listening Conditions

Your company is located in a former high school building, and the large auditorium is used for videoconferences. Presenters stand or sit on the stage, and the video camera operator stands at the back of the room. Rows of large windows, some with drapes, run down two sides of the auditorium. To add brightness to the rooms, all walls and a large partition behind the speakers are painted white.

Viewers sit in the auditorium chairs and watch four televisions that drop from the ceiling at appropriate points. Often, the viewers have trouble understanding what is being said by the presenters.

Recently, viewers have been frustrated because what is seen on television flashes between bright or harsh colors, a blackout, or a long shot of the speaker.

Room problems and recommended corrections: _____

_____

_____

_____

_____

_____

Non-room issues and recommended corrections: _____

_____

_____

_____

_____

Connecting Telephones, Data, and Other Networks

Focus

"Rule No. 1—Please be prompt so your videoconference will start at the designated time. This is especially important if you have scheduled a multipoint videoconference or have arranged for a telephone bridge to be connected to the meeting. Time is valuable to everyone."

—Patrick Carr, Videoconference Network Coordinator
UNISYS

Telephone Connections

Participants in remote locations can be connected to a videoconference through a telephone hook-up, but the problem of limited space at a videoconference site cannot be solved just by adding a telephone connection in a separate room where additional seating is available. You might think that a remote location without a videoconferencing room can simply telephone into the meeting, but it's not quite that easy! While connecting by telephone to a videoconference meeting isn't difficult, there are several issues that must be considered.

Phone Patch

You may have heard the comment, "I'll patch you through" after you have called an office and asked to speak to a specific person. This means that the call is being transferred to another number. Many videoconferencing systems are equipped with a **phone patch,** a peripheral device technically known as a **hybrid telephone interface.** This phone patch creates an electronic connection directly to the audio system for the videoconference. To connect to the videoconference, the caller punches in the telephone number of the line that is connected to the videoconferencing system.

© Photodisc/Getty Images, Inc.

Figure 8-1: In the absence of a phone patch, a speakerphone or teleconference speaker can connect a remote participant.

Acoustical Coupling

While a phone patch is the preferred method for connecting telephone participants to a videoconference, a simplified approach is used in some videoconference rooms. The site videoconference coordinator merely places a speakerphone or a telephone conferencing speaker near the microphone on the videoconference table. This is called **acoustical coupling** because a direct electronic connection to the videoconferencing system does not exist.

In this approach, the caller *hears* what is being said because the presenter talks into the microphone that is situated near the speakerphone or other device. When the caller *talks*, his or her comments are heard over the speakerphone. This is a crude approach that usually introduces audio distortion, room reverberations, and echoes into the conference. It reduces presence, and the telephone participants may have difficulty hearing what is being said in the meeting. With the use of an electronic phone patch, the incoming and outgoing sounds are blended and balanced to reduce or eliminate most of these undesired and distracting effects.

Multipoint Control Unit (MCU) Connection

A speakerphone or phone patch does not work well in a multipoint videoconference that is voice-switched or voice-activated. That's because the electronic equipment cannot distinguish the remote caller's voice over the sounds in the videoconference room to which the phone line is connected. The camera switches to a view of the primary speaker, though the speaker may be in another part of the world. Neither will viewers at the several locations of a multipoint videoconference be able to identify who is talking. If a telephone connection to a videoconference is used, the remote caller should always say his or her name and the calling location.

About 80 percent of videoconferences are multipoint, involving three, four, or more locations. For a multipoint videoconference, the network coordinator asks the remote caller to punch in the telephone number that is connected directly to the phone patch in the videoconferencing bridge or MCU. The remote caller's voice is injected electronically into the meeting and does not activate the video switching system of the MCU. This is the most effective method of connecting a telephone caller to a multipoint videoconference.

Telephone Connection Concerns

You should be aware of other disadvantages of using a phone patch to bring participants into a videoconference. The greatest is the loss of presence. Instead of sounding present with other participants in the videoconference room, some speakers are not only physically remote; they also sound remote. That's because the voices on a telephone connection lack the proper fidelity and range. Telephone callers may have a booming sound caused by the high digital compression on the telephone lines. Here are some precautions to consider:

■ Advise telephone participants, the same as other videoconference participants, to mute or silence their microphones when not talking. This avoids accidental sounds or side conversations that distract the meeting.

■ Do not allow cellular telephones or cordless phones to join the meeting. Although digital cellular telephones are quieter than regular telephone lines, they cannot be muted conveniently.

■ Remember that telephone callers are equal participants in a videoconference. This is easy to forget since they cannot be seen. The meeting host or chairperson should take special care to elaborate on the telephone participant's questions, comments, or other input.

■ Warn telephone callers not to place their conference line on Hold if they leave the room, especially if music is programmed into the Hold function. They should mute the microphone and turn the volume of the speaker down or off.

■ If a telephone bridge is connected to a videoconference room or to an MCU, ask the operator or network coordinator to silence the bridge or telephone multipoint device until all the callers have joined the meeting.

■ Silence all automatic announcements while the telephone bridge is connected to the videoconference; however, if telephone connections are being used, introduce new arrivals so that telephone participants know exactly who is participating in the meeting. ("Samantha Tibez has just joined us here in Chicago.")

■ Remember that telephone callers cannot see who is talking and may be confused regarding who said what. They also may not understand the reason for laughter, especially if it's caused by an action that cannot be seen at remote sites. They could be offended if laughter follows something they say.

■ If an object or visual aid not distributed previously is shown during the videoconference, someone needs to describe it to telephone participants, or they will feel left out of the meeting. This description may seem like a waste of time to participants who can see clearly what is being shown to the group, but it is essential if telephone participants are to understand.

■ Offer to video stream or web cast the videoconference over the computer network to the telephone participants, if feasible. When these PC watchers are using their computers to talk with the videoconference, they must use a headset, as the tiny microphones in a PC or laptop frequently are not strong enough to receive the audio. They should expect to experience a lengthy delay before hearing what the in-room participants will hear immediately. If they try to watch over their PC, but listen over a separate telephone line, the lip synchronization will be lost. This can be extremely frustrating.

Other Considerations

The best-operated videoconferencing rooms expand their capabilities by anticipating the equipment and services that participants may need. If you are in charge of a videoconference, consider the following options.

Figure 8-2: By viewing a web cast and speaking over a telephone, remote participants can be involved in a videoconference.

© Photodisc/Getty Images, Inc.

Using a Fax Machine

Some videoconference rooms are equipped with a fax machine for distributing visuals when the videoconferencing system's graphic camera cannot capture the image. A document can be sent to any site with access to a fax machine. Fax machines also can be used effectively to send last minute agenda changes that were not included in earlier e-mails about the videoconference.

Network Connection

Always provide one local area network (LAN) at any videoconference, so participants can access their departmental server for e-mail and documents they may need during the presentation. Don't forget to provide a 110-volt AC outlet on or near the table, in case of laptop battery failures.

Still Graphics

Slides to be used in a videoconference must always be evaluated to determine whether they comply with TV formatting. Is the type large and bold enough? Do the colors used in the graphic display properly on the videoconference system TV monitors?

Any documents or photos that you plan to present in a videoconference must also be evaluated. Can the graphics camera capture their entire size? Can they be clearly seen when placed under the graphics camera? Nothing beats actually testing the graphics in advance to make sure they are suitably designed.

If you are planning to use the graphics camera for displaying a physical object such as a model or a piece of equipment, make certain that the light near the graphics camera is sufficient for the object to be seen clearly in the videoconferencing monitors. The graphics camera must also have sufficient zoom or close-up capability to adequately show an object. Test the object with the camera before the videoconference!

Finally, if you plan to use the graphics camera as a secondary motion camera, remember that graphics cameras are simple. They are seldom robotic, as is the main motion camera. Be certain the graphics camera is pointed at what is to be shown before you switch to it. Moving the camera around abruptly after you have switched to it can be dizzying to some participants.

Activity 8-1: Making a Recommendation

Mountain Coal Company plans to make a presentation regarding the new vein of coal it has located in the Midwest. Four remote sites will be connecting to one central videoconferencing center. The participation list has grown so large that an overflow room has been set up in another building at the central site.

What telephone connection recommendations would you make in order to provide the best audio at all sites? Should a phone patch be used at all sites, or are speakerphones suitable at some sites? Explain your thinking.

_____

_____

_____

_____

_____

_____

Activity 8-2: Handling Last-Minute Details

A Los Angeles presenter at tomorrow's "Medical Malpractice Update" videoconference arrived by plane last night, but her luggage did not arrive. Several props she expected to display are in her luggage, but she has 8" × 10" illustrations of them with her in her briefcase. One particularly important chart is stored on her home office server. How can you help her solve this dilemma?

_____

_____

_____

_____

_____

_____

Activity 8-3: Setting the Rules

As the leader for an upcoming videoconference at the international temporary agency where you are employed, you decide to prepare a list of Do's and Don'ts regarding the use of telephone connections. Write your list below.

Do's	Don'ts

Delivering a Videoconference

Focus

"Normal meeting skills are employed in videoconferencing, but many people have not developed good meeting skills. Videoconferencing will exaggerate poor meeting procedures. Since one is paying by the hour, it is costly to let a video meeting wander."

—Patrick S. Portway & Carla Lane, Ed.D.
Technical Guide to Teleconferencing & Distance Learning

Participant Protocols

Videoconference participants and observers share the responsibility for assuring a successful conference. The participant **protocols,** appropriate behaviors and practices, listed below should be provided to all attendees before a conference:

- Show up on time, usually about 10 minutes before the scheduled start of the meeting. This allows time for making any final adjustments to your bring-along equipment before the room is connected to the network and also for being seated before the conference begins.

- Avoid side conversations, rattling of papers, and other noises. Turn off your cell phone and pager alarm, especially while the microphones are un-muted and the room is connected to the network. Remember, your nervous pencil tapping on the table could be a distraction to someone 2000 miles away!

- Keep flashing cell phones, laptops, and other blinking lights away from the view of the camera. Otherwise, the CODEC must work harder for no productive purpose.

- Do not place papers or equipment too close to table microphones. In addition to causing operational problems, they may cause equipment to overheat.

- Wait for others to finish speaking and pause for a second before you talk. Be careful not to interrupt. The audio system is fast, but needs a second or two to switch to a new speaker.

- Make certain the room microphones remain muted when no one is talking.

- Refrain from wearing bright or wildly patterned clothing (especially red) or dangling jewelry on the day of the videoconference.

Handling Questions and Answers

When any good presenter finishes speaking, he or she glances around the room and makes eye contact with the audience, then asks in a clear, slow voice, "Are there any questions?" In a videoconference, the speaker asks the question of each remote site attending the meeting. ("Are there any questions from Chicago?") Then the speaker pauses for the remote participants to consider their questions. After all, they may be fumbling with a microphone mute button or making other equipment adjustments.

If the identified site has no question, that's okay, but be sure participants are not experiencing an audio problem that keeps them from asking. Before moving on to the next site, make a comment such as "Since nothing is heard from Chicago, are there any questions from Detroit?" After polling all the participating videoconference sites, poll each of the telephone participants, either by an individual's name or by site.

Finally, if there are any observers, such as those watching a video stream or web cast of the session, and you want to offer them the opportunity to ask questions, instruct them to fax their questions to a fax machine in or near the videoconference room. If one of the participants in your room has a laptop connected to the local area network, questions can also be sent as e-mail or instant messages.

Camera Control Techniques

New users of videoconferencing equipment often fail to use the main motion camera effectively. A little practice with a home video camera is helpful to first-time camera operators.

The ideal view for the camera is a head and shoulders shot of the speaker. This is not a difficult shot; and with just a little practice, most new users find the videoconference main motion camera easy to control. Consider the following suggestions:

■ Most videoconference main motion cameras are controlled robotically, so there is no need for physical lifting or moving of the equipment.

Figure 9-1: A videoconference main motion camera is controlled robotically with a remote device.

- To control the system, most videoconference rooms provide a small, hand-held, infrared remote (IR) control device, similar to the ones used in homes to control a TV, VCR, DVD, CD player, and other entertainment center equipment.

- Most cameras used in videoconferencing are automatically focused (auto-focus) so getting a clear shot is not a concern.

- Videoconference systems usually come with camera pre-sets. These are memory keys that store the positions of the camera. Unless you're in a brand new room, the previous videoconference coordinator has probably already established pre-sets. If not, ask for assistance.

Arranging the Monitors

Most videoconferencing systems have dual monitors—two TV screens. However, not all systems are configured in the same way. For the most effective communications, the following arrangement is recommended:

Figure 9-2: **Videoconference system with dual monitors**

1. The left monitor displays incoming video including:

   - Participants at a remote location

   - Live graphics from a remote location

   - Videotapes from a remote location

2. The right monitor displays outgoing or graphics video including:

   - Participants at your location

   - Stored images, slides, or documents from any location

   - Videotapes from your location

Recording the Session for Evaluation

A videoconference is incomplete until it has been evaluated for effectiveness. Was the speaker compelling? Was the content suitable? Did the technology perform well? Since the network coordinator generally is not responsible for the speakers or the content, this section will focus on the technology. Here are several items to consider for technological evaluation:

- Study the slides and other visual aids to determine whether they were clear and displayed appropriately. Analyze how to improve the slides for the next session.

- Identify which sites provided the best audio and investigate why their sound was better than the sound at other sites.

- Examine how well the main motion cameras and the graphic camera were controlled. Were head and shoulders shots used or were only group views provided? Could participants see who was speaking and observe facial expressions and gestures?

Audio Recording

One of the easiest means to record a videoconference is with a simple voice tape recorder available from electronics stores for about $30. These recorders are often voice activated and do not record unless a sound is made or someone is speaking. An audio recording allows each speaker or the network coordinator to observe how the presentation sounded and to identify distracting noises or distortions. These can be overlooked during a meeting because of a focus on the mechanics of the presentation.

A speaker, for example, may discover, after listening to an audio recording that he or she distorts certain words. One otherwise good speaker recently discovered that he used the expression "irregardless" (there is no such word) when he meant "regardless" or "irrespective." Another speaker realized that she frequently said "um" when she was speaking. These habits can be distracting to other participants, but can be corrected with practice. A careful audio evaluation can help reveal speaking habits that should be corrected.

If you are listening to an audio recording, observe these points:

- How did the speaker, perhaps yourself, respond to questions or disagreements? Were the questions answered fully or did the speaker dodge the issue? Was the speaker defensive or emotional or did the speaker remain logical and objective? If you're the speaker, listening to the audio recording can let you hear how others heard you, rather than how you thought you sounded.

- Can specific questions be followed up, if they were not adequately addressed in the meeting? Can these questions be included in the agenda for the next meeting?

Video Recording

While most videoconference systems are equipped routinely with a VCR, check in advance to make sure one is available. You may need to locate one or bring a blank tape. Generic, inexpensive tapes are adequate. A VCR can record only one video feed at a time; therefore, deciding in advance whether to record incoming or outgoing video is important. Test the VCR to determine if the desired feed is being recorded and to familiarize yourself with the equipment. If you wish to switch video feeds during the course, you will need to be able to make the switch without disrupting the meeting.

Newer videoconference sites often provide a compact disc (CD) recorder. These are commonly called CD-burners because of the heat energy used to make the CD. A CD burner works similarly to a VCR, except that the picture quality may be superior, and you will have a CD instead of a tape at the end of the meeting.

Some videoconference sites have the capability to stream the videoconference session to a computer network server. The session will be recorded on the server and archived there for 30 days or more. If you wish to see a recording of the session, you will be provided with a URL and a password to access the web site or database where the session is stored.

Video recording is especially helpful for evaluating graphics and camera movement. Also, it is a good way to evaluate the appearance of the camera room and participants' clothing to make sure they are not distracting or difficult to see on camera. Just as audio recording can reveal distracting speaking habits, video recording can reveal distracting physical habits, such as swiveling in a chair, twirling a pen, and playing with one's hair. Again, these are habits that can be corrected with practice.

Etiquette and Legalities

A few warnings or precautions are important to remember when making an audio or video recording of a videoconference. Keep these in mind:

- Be aware of any restrictions or limitations imposed by the state and federal governments, such as those pertaining to copyright and privacy. You may need to get permission before you can copy or record certain documents, graphics, art, performances, speeches, or music.

- Before recording any session, either audio or video, notify all participants that the meeting will be recorded. Don't forget to advise participants who join the meeting late and may not have heard an earlier announcement.

- Bear in mind that some VCR units will continue to record the audio from the videoconference site, even though the site's microphones are muted. In one particularly embarrassing incident, a videoconference manager asked an employee at another site to record the incoming video for later evaluation of the presentation at the far-end. Without reviewing the recorded tape, the employee sent it to the manager. Unfortunately, it contained side comments and jokes made during the meeting. Although these weren't heard at other sites during the meeting, they were recorded by the VCR, and the manager heard each one.

Activity 9-1: Listing Responsibilities of Participants

 Make a list of the ways that participants who do not have a speaking role can add to the success or failure of a videoconference.

Things that can help a videoconference	Things that can hurt a videoconference

Activity 9-2: Fielding Questions

Assume a presenter has finished the main portion of her talk. Write the dialogue she should use to allow participants to ask questions from sites in Los Angeles, Houston, St. Louis, and Miami.

_____

_____

_____

_____

_____

Activity 9-3: Exploring Recording Restrictions

To learn more about copyright restrictions, visit the U.S. Copyright Office online at www.copyright.gov. Search the site for issues related to videoconferencing and teleconferencing, and write a brief summary of the results. How would these issues affect the audio or video recording of a videoconference?

_____

_____

_____

_____

_____

_____

Delivering a Videoconference

Activity 9-4: Evaluating Videoconferences

Answer the following questions about evaluation techniques and procedures for a videoconference.

1. What evaluation information can be gained from an audio recording of a videoconference?

_____

_____

_____

2. What evaluation information can be gained from a video recording of a videoconference?

_____

_____

_____

3. What are the advantages and disadvantages of audio recording for evaluation and video recording for evaluation?

Advantages of audio recording _____

_____

Disadvantages of audio recording _____

_____

Advantages of video recording _____

_____

Disadvantages of video recording _____

_____

A Few Final Recommendations

Focus

"Is it time for business people to change their meeting behavior? Video-conferencing saves time because you don't have to travel; it saves money, and increases the impact of communications. This changing behavior is not just about your pocketbook. It is about the acceptance of the technology like we accept e-mail."

—Christine Perey, President
Perey Research

Take Lessons from the Past

Network videoconferencing coordinators often conduct surveys of participants after a conference. One primary purpose of the surveys is to determine what improvements can be made to use technology more effectively in future conferences. Since some network videoconferencing coordinators have assisted and supported meetings for years, they can be valuable assets in your learning and preparation. If you are leading a video-conference, contact the network coordinator and obtain the results of any previous surveys. You will learn about common mistakes and how to avoid them in your sessions.

Local site videoconferencing coordinators can be helpful also. Although their experience is often more limited than the experience of the network coordinators, they have seen all types of sessions—from the best to the worst. They know valuable tips to help you get off to a good start using the videoconferencing technology, and they may have equipment literature or brochures for you to study.

To make certain you understand what procedures and protocols are expected from users of the videoconference center, talk to other individuals, both inside and outside your organization who have conducted videoconferences previously. Discuss your plans with previous users and ask if they can offer advice. For example, you may:

■ Ask how they could have improved the meeting.

■ Ask if they were pleased with their slides. If they still have a copy, examine them carefully to see if you can improve upon them.

Conducting Research

Contact the manufacturer of the videoconference system you will be using. Often, manufacturers provide booklets or white papers on their technology and suggest innovative presentation approaches that will make your meeting more interesting and informative.

Log on to the Internet and do a search under "videoconferences," "meetings," and related topics. Get warmed up by reading about your equipment, so you will feel comfortable with the technology and its uses. Manufacturers such as Tandberg (www.tandbergusa.com) and SKC Communication (www.skc.com) have informative web sites with features, such as product demos, glossaries of key terms, and free newsletters. Check booksellers on the Internet. Do a search under "meetings" and related topics to see what current books may be available in print. If you pick up one good idea, it will be worth the effort and expense.

If your organization has a communications department, it may already have well-established guidelines and tips for conducting effective meetings. The department may also offer classes or online training to help you develop your meeting management and presentation skills.

Inviting Guest Speakers

Outside consultants or internal subject experts can be valuable additions to a meeting. When one of these guest speakers doesn't have access to a videoconference room at his or her location, ask the speaker to travel to a nearby public or private site that you will set up for the presentation. Sprint Video Conferencing[SM] and Kinko's[®] have combined services to offer hundreds of such rooms in Kinko's stores across the country. Additionally, public video conference rooms are available in many universities and public libraries.

If a rented videoconference room is not feasible for a guest speaker, connect the speaker to the videoconference meeting via the telephone line in his or her office. The speaker can provide visual materials to the participants via Microsoft NetMeeting[®], or he or she can send Microsoft PowerPoint[®] slides via e-mail to you. You can display the slides on cue during the conference.

If the guest speaker is unable to actually participate in the videoconference, ask him or her to prepare a videotape that you can play during your conference. If the main issue is a schedule conflict, prepare a separate videoconference just between yourself and the speaker, then ask any questions you would expect to be raised in the actual meeting. Record the videoconference for playback later during your meeting. If possible, bring the speaker back live into the actual meeting at the conclusion of the tape—perhaps for a short question and answer period.

Before the meeting, brief the guest speaker on what is expected. Answer all of his or her questions fully, and do everything you can to make the person feel comfortable. Be sure to send a note of appreciation before *and* after the session. Some speakers wish to distribute copies of previous presentations or papers they have written. Distribute these with the meeting announcement, so other participants will be better prepared.

Use a Planning Checklist

Make copies of the checklist below for your files. Each time you are designated to lead or participate in a videoconference meeting, tape a copy of the checklist to your planning folder. Place a checkmark by each item as you complete it during your planning.

Pre-Planning

☐ Contact the video coordinator for information about dates the videoconference room will be available.

☐ Schedule the meeting months or a year ahead of time.

☐ Confirm all speakers and presenters.

☐ Notify participants several times of the date, time, and length of the meeting.

☐ Discuss the meeting objectives with all presenters.

☐ Arrange for all necessary equipment.

Preparations before the Meeting

☐ Confirm the attendance of all non-presenting participants and observers.

☐ Prepare and send out advance copies of the agenda and other preliminary material.

☐ Develop interesting and informational visual aids.

　　Use large, boldface type.

　　Provide good spacing and placement.

Refrain from overcrowding the words.

Use clear, readable graphics and charts.

☐ Test all equipment.

Preparations on the Day of the Meeting

☐ Re-test all equipment.

☐ Begin and end the meeting on time.

☐ Get acquainted by introducing yourself and the other participants.

☐ Face the participants and speak naturally.

☐ Engage the participants in the discussion.

☐ Act naturally. Don't dress, talk, or act differently than in a normal face-to-face meeting.

☐ Relax and enjoy your videoconference.

Follow-up Procedures

☐ Contact several of the participants or survey all the participants and ask their opinion of the videoconference.

☐ Request suggestions for improving the next meeting.

☐ Use questions about the conference as clues to what additional information is needed in future announcements. For example:

Did any of the participants need better directions to the nearest videoconference room?

Do other videoconference sites need to be added to the meeting?

Activity 10-1: Gathering Information

Imagine that you work for a pet food company and have been designated as the leader of a videoconference for veterinarians on the topic of animal shelters. You have been given the names of your company's network coordinator and leaders of two previous videoconferences. They have all volunteered to offer any guidance you need for your upcoming conference. On a separate sheet of paper, prepare a list of questions you would like to ask them before you start planning your conference.

Activity 10-2: Establishing a Schedule

Today's date is January 12, 200x, and the videoconference you will lead in Activity 10-1 needs to occur sometime in the next 12 months. Prepare a list of tasks showing the date or the date and time you will accomplish each task in planning, preparing for, delivering, and following-up the conference. Refer to the checklist on pages 82–83 as you make your plans. For your convenience, a year-at-a-glance calendar is provided on the next page.

Tasks	Date/Time

A Few Final Recommendations

January

S	M	T	W	T	F	S
		1	2	3	4	
5	6	7	8	9	10	11
12	13	14	15	16	17	18
19	20	21	22	23	24	25
26	27	28	29	30	31	

February

S	M	T	W	T	F	S
					1	
2	3	4	5	6	7	8
9	10	11	12	13	14	15
16	17	18	19	20	21	22
23	24	25	26	27	28	

March

S	M	T	W	T	F	S
						1
2	3	4	5	6	7	8
9	10	11	12	13	14	15
16	17	18	19	20	21	22
23	24	25	26	27	28	29
30	31					

April

S	M	T	W	T	F	S
		1	2	3	4	5
6	7	8	9	10	11	12
13	14	15	16	17	18	19
20	21	22	23	24	25	26
27	28	29	30			

May

S	M	T	W	T	F	S
				1	2	3
4	5	6	7	8	9	10
11	12	13	14	15	16	17
18	19	20	21	22	23	24
25	26	27	28	29	30	31

June

S	M	T	W	T	F	S
1	2	3	4	5	6	7
8	9	10	11	12	13	14
15	16	17	18	19	20	21
22	23	24	25	26	27	28
29	30					

July

S	M	T	W	T	F	S
		1	2	3	4	5
6	7	8	9	10	11	12
13	14	15	16	17	18	19
20	21	22	23	24	25	26
27	28	29	30	31		

August

S	M	T	W	T	F	S
					1	2
3	4	5	6	7	8	9
10	11	12	13	14	15	16
17	18	19	20	21	22	23
24	25	26	27	28	29	30
31						

September

S	M	T	W	T	F	S
	1	2	3	4	5	6
7	8	9	10	11	12	13
14	15	16	17	18	19	20
21	22	23	24	25	26	27
28	29	30				

October

S	M	T	W	T	F	S
			1	2	3	4
5	6	7	8	9	10	11
12	13	14	15	16	17	18
19	20	21	22	23	24	25
26	27	28	29	30	31	

November

S	M	T	W	T	F	S
						1
2	3	4	5	6	7	8
9	10	11	12	13	14	15
16	17	18	19	20	21	22
23	24	25	26	27	28	29
30						

December

S	M	T	W	T	F	S
	1	2	3	4	5	6
7	8	9	10	11	12	13
14	15	16	17	18	19	20
21	22	23	24	25	26	27
28	29	30	31			

A Few Final Recommendations

Activity 10-3: Inviting the Guest Speaker

For the videoconference in Activity 10-1, you have decided to invite a guest expert, who lives in Lebanon, Tennessee, a small town about 30 miles from Nashville. The town is about 200 miles from Memphis and about 150 miles from Knoxville. The speaker cannot attend your conference but has agreed to travel to a public videoconference room.

Search the Internet to locate a public videoconference room you will recommend to the speaker, then determine the cost for a two-hour presentation, and compare this cost to the cost of traveling to attend a meeting in person. Make a list of items you will need to discuss with the speaker.

Web sites visited: _____

_____

_____

Public videoconference room recommended: _____

_____

_____

Cost of two-hour videoconference presentation: _____

Estimated costs of traveling to attend meeting in person: _____

_____

_____

_____

Items to discuss with speaker: _____

_____

_____

_____

_____

A Few Final Recommendations

Videoconference Planning Checklist

Pre-Planning

- [ ] Contact the video coordinator for information about dates the videoconference room will be available.
- [ ] Schedule the meeting months or a year ahead of time.
- [ ] Confirm all speakers and presenters.
- [ ] Notify participants several times of the date, time, and length of the meeting.
- [ ] Discuss the meeting objectives with all presenters.
- [ ] Arrange for all necessary equipment.

Preparations before the Meeting

- [ ] Confirm the attendance of all non-presenting participants and observers.
- [ ] Prepare and send out advance copies of the agenda and other preliminary material.
- [ ] Develop interesting and informational visual aids.

    Use large, boldface type.   - [ ] Refrain from overcrowding the words.

    Provide good spacing and placement.   - [ ] Use clear, readable graphics and charts.

- [ ] Test all equipment.

Preparations on the Day of the Meeting

- [ ] Re-test all equipment.
- [ ] Begin and end the meeting on time.
- [ ] Get acquainted by introducing yourself and the other participants.
- [ ] Face the participants and speak naturally.
- [ ] Engage the participants in the discussion.
- [ ] Act naturally. Don't dress, talk, or act differently than in a normal face-to-face meeting.
- [ ] Relax and enjoy your videoconference.

Follow-up Procedures

- [ ] Contact several of the participants or survey all the participants and ask their opinion of the videoconference.
- [ ] Request suggestions for improving the next meeting.
- [ ] Use questions about the conference as clues to what additional information is needed in future announcements. For example:

    Did any of the participants need better directions to the nearest videoconference room?

    Do other videoconference sites need to be added to the meeting?

Glossary

acoustical coupling—a simplified approach to connecting a remote participant in which a speakerphone or a telephone conferencing speaker is placed near the microphone on the videoconference table

agenda—a list of topics to be discussed or order of business to be followed in a meeting

analog signals—complex electronic signals of varying frequency and amplitude that produce high quality audio and video

audio output—sound production

chairman controlled—a videoconference in which only one person, the presenter, is seen

chroma—color scheme or information

CODEC—short for Coder/Decoder, a specialized computer that converts analog signals to digital data

coding—the conversion from analog to digital signals; another name for digitalization

compression algorithms—more efficient, standardized software programs to handle video communications

continuous presence—a videoconference that allows all individuals in attendance at a meeting to be viewed at all times

data conference—in addition to communicating with audio and video, a data conference allows participants to exchange graphics, transfer files, and use a text-based chat program

default shot—an image of the videoconference room that is shown throughout the entire session. Usually, this is a long-range, wide-angle view of the room or sometimes a close-up view of the location's name sign

digital circuits—special telephone lines that send television programs and two-way video signals around the country

digital data—data transmitted as a string of 0s and 1s that can be read by a computer; produces lower quality audio and video signals that can be transmitted faster and more economically

digitalization—the conversion from analog to digital signals; another name for coding

digital network—technology that allows for the more economical and efficient exchange of information across a group of connected computers and phone lines

gateway—an electronic device that connects VoIP and ISDN networks and allows them to operate as one network

graphics camera—a special TV camera with a short focal length lens that points straight down to the conference table surface. The camera serves the same purpose as the overhead projector that speakers use for their clear plastic slides in a conventional presentation.

H.320—ITU designation for videoconferencing switched network

H.323—ITU designation for Internet-based videoconference networks

hybrid network—a network that uses both VoIP and ISDN digital networks

hybrid telephone Interface—a peripheral device also known as a phone patch. This device creates an electronic connection directly to the audio system for the videoconference. To connect to the videoconference, a telephone participant punches in the telephone number of the line that is connected to the videoconferencing system.

Integrated Services Digital Network (ISDN)—a phone company standard for digital transmission over ordinary telephone copper wire as well as over other media

Glossary

ITU—International Telecommunications Union, the 136-year-old UN-sponsored international organization that creates cooperative standards for telecommunications systems

loop-back—previewing slides or other images after they have come through the CODEC process

magenta effect—color blending or chroma distortion that takes place when translating a PC image to a TV image

multipoint control unit (MCU)—a complex electronic system needed to connect multiple locations and conduct a multipoint videoconference; another name for videoconference bridge

multipoint videoconference—a videoconference involving more than two locations

network architecture—a digital system of connected phone lines and computers; another name for network design

network coordinator—the individual responsible for operating the videoconference bridge or MCU during a videoconference

network design—a digital system of connected phone lines and computers; another name for network architecture

phone patch—a peripheral device also known as a hybrid telephone interface. This device creates an electronic connection directly to the audio system for the videoconference. To connect to the videoconference, a telephone participant punches in the telephone number of the line that is connected to the videoconferencing system.

point-to-point—a videoconference between only two locations

presence—the perception or feeling that a person talking in a videoconference is actually present in the room

pre-sets—camera positions that are stored in the memory of a videoconference system

protocols—appropriate behaviors and practices in a videoconference

public videoconference room—videoconference facilities and equipment available for rent from phone companies, public libraries, and other service providers

scan converter—a device that changes a PC image of the slide to a TV quality image

videoconference bridge—a complex electronic system needed to connect multiple locations and conduct a multipoint videoconference; another name for multipoint control unit

videoconferencing switched network—the system of using a CODEC to dial up a videoconferencing location

Video over Internet Protocol (VoIP)—Internet-based videoconference networks

voice-switched videoconference—a videoconference in which only the person speaking or that speaker's location can be seen on screen. Also called voice-activated.

video streaming—one-way video and audio from a videoconference sent over a data network

videoconferencing—the use of digital video and audio technology for two-way communication across long distances

web cast—one-way audio or audio and video viewed over a data network such as the Internet

zoom—extending a camera lens for a close-up view of a videoconference participant

Index